SEVEN SEASONED PLAYERS INSTRUCT YOU STEP-BY-STEP IN WHAT THEY DO BEST:

Billy Casper "sees" the fairway wood shot to make a birdie, and uses the long iron—the most difficult club in the bag

•

Bruce Crampton plays off the tee, making maximum use of the driver, then gets the ball close to the pin with a favorite mid-iron

•

Bob Goalby handles the difficult approach and trouble shot the way the pros do

•

Jim Ferree makes playing in sand look easy and talks about the long putter— for the first time in *any* golf instruction book!

•

Gene Littler tackles putting with the traditional putter and "plumb" putting, the technique favored by the finest amateurs and the greatest pros

•

Bobby Nichols shows you the correct grip and correct stance

•

Bob Watson gets the best from the short irons and tells the secret of putting a backspin on the ball with the seven-, eight-, and nine-irons

PLAYING WITH THE PROS

"RECOMMENDED . . . GREAT PHOTOGRAPHY TO GO WITH GOLF TIPS FROM LEADING PROS OF THE SENIOR TOUR."   —*Chattanooga Times*

JOHN COYNE is the editor of *Better Golf* and *New Golf for Women* and has written extensively on golf for magazines including *Inside Golf, Golf Digest,* and *Travel & Leisure.* He is also the author of the national bestsellers *The Piercing* and *The Legacy.*

JULES ALEXANDER is one of the most respected golf photographers in the United States. His work includes two books of photography, *Philippine Hospitality* and *St. Andrews Golf Club—Birthplace of American Golf.*

WITH THE

PROS
Golf Lessons from the Senior Tour

BY JOHN COYNE
WITH PHOTOGRAPHY BY
JULES ALEXANDER

A PLUME BOOK

PLUME
Published by the Penguin Group
Penguin Books USA Inc., 375 Hudson Street, New York, New York 10014, U.S.A.
Penguin Books Ltd, 27 Wrights Lane, London W8 5TZ, England
Penguin Books Australia Ltd, Ringwood, Victoria, Australia
Penguin Books Canada Ltd, 10 Alcorn Avenue, Toronto, Ontario, Canada M4V 3B2
Penguin Books (N.Z.) Ltd, 182-190 Wairau Road, Auckland 10, New Zealand

Penguin Books Ltd, Registered Offices: Harmondsworth, Middlesex, England

Published by Plume, an imprint of New American Library, a division of Penguin
Books USA Inc. Previously published in a Dutton edition.

First Plume Printing, May, 1992
10 9 8 7 6 5 4 3 2 1

℗ REGISTERED TRADEMARK—MARCA REGISTRADA

LIBRARY OF CONGRESS CATALOGING-IN-PUBLICATION DATA
Coyne, John.
    Playing with the pros : golf lessons from the senior tour / by
John Coyne ; photographs by Jules Alexander.
        p.   cm.
    ISBN 0-452-26802-8
    1. Golf.   I. Title.
GV965.C688   1992
796.352—dc20   91-40317
                                                        CIP

Printed in the United States of America
Original hardcover design by Barbara Huntley

BOOKS ARE AVAILABLE AT QUANTITY DISCOUNTS WHEN USED TO PROMOTE PRODUCTS OR SERVICES. FOR IN-
FORMATION PLEASE WRITE TO PREMIUM MARKETING DIVISION, PENGUIN BOOKS USA INC., 375 HUDSON
STREET, NEW YORK, NEW YORK 10014.

For Michael McNulty and Michael McCaskey
. . . still trying to break par

Contents

Acknowledgments

I would like to thank Tim Crosby, Media Director of the PGA Senior Tour, for his help, and the tournament directors of the Northville Long Island Classic, Newport Cup, and the Premier Championship for their cooperation. I would also like to thank Steven Frei of ProServ, Inc., and Kevin Mulroy of New American Library for his interest and encouragement. Special thanks to Barbara Huntley for her book design.

PLAYING WITH THE PROS
Golf Lessons from the Senior Tour

Introduction
by Harry Cooper

I've been teaching people how to play golf since I was eighteen years old. I'm eighty-five now and in all these years of playing and watching others play, I haven't seen much change in the golf swing. Oh, the equipment has changed tremendously, but not the basic swing. The same golf fundamentals are still being taught.

Every once in a while someone puts a new name on the basic swing. They'll call it the inverted C or the Square-to-Square, but it is still the same swing that we're all trying to perfect.

It is certainly true that there have been tremendous changes in the equipment. When I first started to play down in Texas, we had to put together our set of clubs. In fact, I was the second-to-last professional to shift from wood to steel shafts. Max Smith, I know, was the very last.

At the time—and this would be in the Twenties—one had to put together a "set" of clubs, for there were no two clubs that were just alike. It wasn't until the early Thirties when they developed a system of golf club uniformity. Before then you might have ten mashie-niblicks and not two of them had the same loft. So we put together the best set of clubs by picking and choosing, and we went out and played on the PGA Tour.

It wasn't much of a tour then. In fact, during the Depression the PGA actually gave up on it, thinking no one would come out to see a bunch of pros play golf. At the time, Fred Corcoran was the tournament director for the PGA and when about twenty-five of us got together and resigned from the organization, we hired Fred to continue the tournament for us.

Well, when the PGA learned this, they decided to go ahead with the tour, and we agreed, and that became the PGA Tour that we have today.

I'm often asked, Who do I think is the greatest golfer? and I guess I'd have to say Jack Nicklaus. He has a great swing, and he has had great success. He's a strong player and he swings open to close, which I agree with one hundred percent. His teacher in his early years was a man named Jack Grout, and I myself knew Jack when I was a home professional in Chicago. In fact, Jack used to take lessons from me.

Another one of Nicklaus's teachers was Byron Nelson. Byron and I, of course, played against each other on tour years ago. I remember giving him a lesson once. At that time, they called me "Pipeline" because I hit the ball pretty damn straight. Well, Bryon came to me at the Masters in Augusta and asked me how I did it. How did I hit the ball so straight?

I went through the whole rigmarole, telling him how I set up, what I did. A year later he came back, again at the Masters, and he said, "I've got your secret."

I said, "What is it?" and Byron said, "Well, you keep your club on the line longer than anybody else."

I smiled and said, Well, that's what I told you a year ago.

That is the one thing players don't do today: keep the club on the line after they hit the ball.

Keeping the ball in the fairway is what this game is all about. You watch a tournament on television and half those fellows are off in the rough. I was looking at some old clips awhile back, and I noticed that some reporters during the Twenties and Thirties used to call me "The Machine," just like they called Gene Littler a few years ago. We're both the same kind of player. We keep the ball on the fairway. We keep it in play.

Now, the reason most people don't keep the ball in play is that they make a basic mistake. The average golfer leads from his right shoulder. But if you lead the swing from the point of the left hip—going to first base, for example, instead of third base—you automatically keep the right shoulder back.

Another common mistake most beginning golfers make is that they don't take lessons and establish the fundamentals of the swing. They just go out any old way and do their own thing. If you want to play this game right, you have to get the fundamentals set in your mind. Then you have to practice, work at your swing, and wait for your swing to come to you. In time you'll find out that you have a natural swing. Or at least it will feel natural to you.

I believe anyone with normal athletic skills can become a good player. My friend Ben Hogan said much the same thing. His point was, I believe, that anyone with normal coordination and strength, who has the time, can shoot in the 70s. That's true enough.

The secret of this game really is the person himself. Golf is so complex to start with and there are so many little things that might go wrong, it can seem overwhelming. The answer is getting the fundamentals right and then going out and working on them.

But the crux of the swing is getting to the point where you understand what you're doing with your hands. Your hands alone control the face of the club. If you can control the face of the club, you can control the direction the ball will travel.

I teach everyone to hit the ball with a slightly open stance. I like the idea of hitting out to the line, never around to it.

Here's a little practice tip that is useful to everyone, and one I use when I give a golf lesson:

I point out three spots in the distance and tell the player to line up for those three shots—using a driver and a ball. I don't have them hit the ball, just line up so they can see for themselves where they're aiming. It has been my experience that no more than one or two players in a hundred will be on the correct line. The majority will have set themselves up ten to two hundred yards to the right of their target.

Now, the reason they will be aiming right rather than left is because most of them are using their bodies to line up the shot. They'll look over their left shoulder and not position their feet correctly.

There is a simple way to correct that mistake. First, before hitting any shot, stand directly behind the ball and then walk up and hit it. If anyone has ever watched Jack Nicklaus play, they'll see that he does exactly that.

What you want to do is stand behind the ball and get the correct line. You want to draw an imaginary line from the ball toward the target and on to infinity. (Fig. 1.)

Next, you boil all that down to six inches in front of the ball and six inches behind it. That's your line! That's part of the overall line. You focus on that one-foot line and when you swing, you carry your club through that line.

Once I'm over the ball, I look up only for a second, take

(Fig. 1.) *Light Horse Harry Cooper, still playing and teaching the game of golf.*

a glance at the target to reaffirm what I already know about the distance to the target, but I keep my concentration on the one-foot line.

I always try to be oblivious to everything on the right or left of me when I'm over the ball, and I very seldom knock a ball out of bounds.

I remember one time that I did let my concentration falter, at the Canadian Open in 1938. I had already won that open twice, and I was coming up to the 18th hole with another win in sight. All I needed was a 6 on the par 4 to win the tournament.

I had a big gallery, all on the right side, and there was a fence going down the left side and it was out-of-bounds. I got set to hit my drive the first time and some fellow ran out from the gallery, so I had to stop and start over again.

Well, I went through my usual procedure of setting myself up, looking at the line, concentrating on that one foot of distance before and after the ball, and got set a second time. And just then the same fellow ran out of the gallery again. So I stopped once more. But when I went back to play, I didn't do my usual setup routine. I was in a rush to get off the tee, to finish the round, and I knocked the ball out-of-bounds. I took a 7 on that final hole, and then lost to Sam Snead in a playoff. But there would have never been a playoff if I had remembered my setup routine.

There's another routine that is important to anyone who plays golf, and it will help speed up play, which, I think, upsets people who play more than hitting a bad shot.

After you hit the ball, don't fuss about how badly you played it. Train yourself to think immediately of the next shot. What are you going to do now? Think of the next shot as you walk to the ball, or wait for your playing partners to hit. Learn to concentrate on what kind of shot you'll play next. Then when you reach the ball, you'll be ready to play. The less you fuss and worry, the better you'll play.

Golf is not an easy game to play, but it is a rewarding one. It is the only sport where anyone, regardless of skill or age or handicap, can at one time or the other hit a golf ball just like a professional. Just like a Nicklaus or Palmer.

And having hit the ball just once like a pro makes us all

want to come out to the golf course and play again. That's why golf is such a great sport. And a sport for a lifetime.

I tell the young people I teach who are playing football and hockey and all those other physical sports that they're likely to wind up with an injury, and that they won't be able to play the sport once they leave school. But if they play golf there is less chance of getting hurt, and a bigger chance they'll play the game for the rest of their lives. So all you parents get your son or daughter off the playing field and onto the golf course.

Look at me! I'm approaching the end of my eighties, and I still believe that one of these days soon I'll lick this game. If I can do it at eighty-five, then you can, too!

A Brief History of
the Senior Tour

The Senior PGA Tour is considered to be one of the most successful sports ventures of the 1980s. It is thought that the idea for such a tour might have originated at the 1963 Masters, when Gene Sarazen told Fred Raphael, creator of the Liberty Mutual Legends of Golf, "The young legend Arnold Palmer is paired with the old legend Gene Sarazen."

From that comment, Raphael, a pioneer in televised golf who directed the "Shell's Wonderful World of Golf" show, orchestrated the first made-for-television Legends of Golf in 1978. A thrilling six-hole playoff one year later involving Julius Boros and Roberto De Vicenzo against Art Wall and Tommy Bolt captured the public's attention and spurred the birth of senior golf.

Then in January of 1980, the idea for senior golf took a giant leap forward when a handful of former PGA Tour players met to consider whether such a tour might be possible. They believed they could arrange a few events for "seniors" if they could find sponsors and have the

PGA Tour direct the tournaments. This would be a year-long tour, not just special events like the Legends of Golf and the PGA Seniors Championship.

At that meeting on January 16, 1980, were the inner circle of golfing greats: Sam Snead, Julius Boros, Gardner Dickinson, Bob Goalby, Don January, and Dan Sikes—all of them leaders of the career money list on the PGA Tour.

These players knew that any senior tour would have to trade on the reputations and images made by PGA Tour players over their long years of touring. Eligibility criteria were therefore centered around a player's position on the career money list and number of career victories. It was also determined that such a senior tour could succeed only with a format emphasizing pro-am play. A format for play was set with a field of fifty players (later expanded to seventy-two) and two rounds of pro-am play.

A Senior PGA Tour was approved by the PGA Tour a few days later, on January 22, 1980, and work began immediately to establish events for Senior Tour play. Two tournaments were held in 1980, one in Atlantic City and the other in Melbourne, Florida.

From this point on, the Senior Tour began to grow. In 1981 there were five events. In 1982 the number had jumped to eleven, and by 1983 it had reached eighteen. In 1990 forty-one tournaments are scheduled.

The Senior Tour plays on many of the finest courses in the United States. Don January captured his twenty-sixth Senior Tour crown at La Coasta Country Club, becoming the first player to win the regular Tour MONY Tournament of Champions and the Senior version of the same event. Dale Douglass garnered his first Senior Tour victory at the prestigious Vintage Club, Bruce Crampton won his sixth of seven tournaments in 1986 at the Desert Inn course in Las Vegas, and Bob Charles teamed with LPGA member Amy

Alcott to win the Mazda Champions at the lush paradise of Jamaica's Tryall Golf and Beach Club.

Prize money for the tour has grown even more dramatically than the number of events. In the first year the total prize money was $250,000. In 1990 the official money reached fourteen million dollars.

"It's unbelievable," says Billy Casper. "If anyone had told me five years ago I'd be playing in a forty-one-tournament circuit with fourteen million in prize money, I'd have said they were crazy. But we are not only playing for more money than we ever did in our lives, but we're also having the time of our lives."

A player must be fifty years of age to qualify for the Senior Tour, and then either have to be exempted by the individual tournament or gain a spot through the National Qualifying Tournament. In 1990 the starting field was increased from seventy-two to seventy-eight.

In addition to the Senior Tour, there is a special Super Seniors competition for players sixty years old and above. This is a two-day event within the regular forty-five-hole tournament.

Television coverage has kept up with the growing interest in the new tour. Twenty-one events are now on national television, including nine tournaments on major networks.

Bob Goalby, who was at the first planning meeting, believes that the Senior Tour has become almost "too successful." He thinks that the touring pros now have more tournaments than they really want. "We're older and we don't want to play as much." Also, some of the new players coming on tour are not regulars from the PGA Tour. According to Goalby, "We have lawyers and doctors, steelworkers, all wanting to be on the Senior Tour. Wherever I'm traveling around the country, I have a good amateur player come up to me and say he's thinking of quitting his profession to join the Senior Tour. They all have visions of being another Palmer or Sam Snead."

Goalby and other former regulars on the PGA Tour know that it will become increasingly difficult for such players to make the Senior Tour. "When we started the Senior Tour in 1980, we had quit playing competitive golf at forty and forty-five," Goalby remarked. "We were all out to pasture. Sam Snead had been out of tournament golf for ten years. Others just as long. (Fig. 1.)

"We got started and the regular tour guys laughed at us. Who would want to watch a bunch of old, gray-haired guys? Well, we proved them wrong, and now they can't wait until they turn fifty and join our tour."

These "old" golfers, the great legends of the Fifties—Palmer, Casper, Crampton, Littler, Goalby—found that there was an audience who wanted to see them play competitive golf once more. Soon, Gary Player was predicting that the Senior Tour would outshine the regular PGA Tour in terms of money and fan interest.

The new Senior Tour has certainly prolonged the golf lives of many players for another ten to fifteen years. As Chi Chi Rodriguez has said, "Where else can you turn fifty and have a job waiting for you? All I know is that my fortieth birthday was a lot harder than my fiftieth." (Fig. 2.)

Unique personalities characterize the Senior Tour: Rodriguez's matador performance, Arnold Palmer scoring holes-in-one on consecutive days on the same hole, and Jim Ferree becoming one of the top putters with his fifty-inch long putter. They all give the Senior Tour something special.

"I see no limitation on how far the Senior Tour can go," said Arnold Palmer, who has won seventy times on the Senior and regular tours. "Our growth has been tremen-

(Fig. 1.) Gary Player, one of the all-time greats, a dominant player on the Senior Tour.

(Fig. 2.) *Chi Chi Rodriguez has found his greatest success on the Senior Tour.*

dous the last seven years, and its only going to get better in the future.'' (Fig. 3.)

If nothing else, the Senior Tour has proven what golfers have always known, that golf is a game for one's lifetime.

(Fig. 3.) The legend himself, Arnold Palmer, still winning tournaments as he reaches sixty.

It is not just a sport for the young, to be given up when one leaves college or is too old to play against young legs and young heart.

Golf as it is played on the new Senior Tour proves that these golfing legends may get older and grayer, but they never lose their game or their competitive spirit.

BOBBY NICHOLS

BIRTHDATE: April 14, 1936

BIRTHPLACE: Louisville, Kentucky

RESIDENCE: Fort Myers, Florida

JOINED PGA TOUR: 1960

PGA TOUR VICTORIES: 11

PGA TOUR CAREER EARNINGS: $993,005

JOINED SENIOR PGA TOUR: 1986

SENIOR TOUR VICTORIES THROUGH 1989: 1

SENIOR TOUR EARNINGS THROUGH 1989: $480,310

CAREER EARNINGS: $1,473,315

BEST YEAR ON PGA TOUR: 1964

BEST YEAR ON SENIOR PGA TOUR: $226,936 (1988)

BOBBY NICHOLS

The Comeback Kid

Bobby Nichols is one of golf's great "comeback" kids. In high school in Louisville, Kentucky, he suffered a critical injury in an automobile accident that left him paralyzed from the waist down and unconscious for thirteen days. Three months later, when he was released from the hospital, he had regained the use of his legs and still could play golf. He went on to become the junior golf champ of the state and also to play football at Texas A&M. In 1962 he won the Ben Hogan Award from the Golf Writers for his courageous comeback from this serious injury.

Then in 1975 he was hurt again, this time by lightning at the Western Open. He was one of a half-dozen players and caddies struck by a bolt of lightning that leapfrogged across the Chicago golf course. Lee Trevino was also hurt in this storm.

Nichols turned professional in 1960, and four years later he beat Jack Nicklaus and Arnold Palmer by three shots to win the 1964 PGA Championship at Columbus, Ohio. He went on to win a total of eleven PGA Tour events before joining the Senior Tour in 1986, and began his new golf career by winning the Showdown Classic in his first year. In 1988, he earned more money than any other non-winner, and last year finished twenty-two in the money list, and earned $210,097. (Fig.1.)

(Fig. 1.) *Bobby Nichols came from near tragedy to the PGA Tour.*

Bobby Nichols is part of the second generation of players to move from the regular tour onto the Senior Tour. For him the Senior Tour has been a "mulligan in life."

"We were never able to play during my time on the PGA Tour for the kind of money we're getting today on the Senior Tour," Nichols remarks, grateful to the players who conceived of the idea for such a tour and made it happen. "For me it has meant I have a second chance to compete, to be active, and to do what I enjoy doing most, playing golf."

In addition to the tournament itself, Nicholas added, "The Senior Tour has provided many pros the opportunity to do corporate golf outings as well as clinics, exhibitions, and one-day charitable events."

Most of the seniors, like Nichols, enjoy the pro-amateur events that precede the golf tournaments. According to Nichols, "The amateurs from corporations are the backbone of the Senior Tour. They put up the money that guarantees the prizes."

Turning fifty and returning to competition on the Senior Tour, Nichols finds that maintaining his concentration is his most difficult battle. "I find it is hard to keep my concentration through a round of golf, and over the length of the tournament."

While Nichols admits that he doesn't strike the ball as far as he once did and that he doesn't putt quite as well, he is able to make up for some of these failings through his knowledge of the game and course management. With these skills, plus new golf equipment and being in good physical shape, he's still a competitive player, and professional golf is still his game. (Fig. 2.)

(Fig. 2.) Winner of the Southwestern Bell Classic in 1989,
Nichols plans to continue playing on the Senior Tour well
into the 1990s.

Playing with
the Correct Grip

The golf swing begins with the correct grip. It is the foundation of the swing and the starting point to play the game. If the grip is wrong, it is unlikely that anyone can become a good golfer. One nice aspect of golf is that basically the same grip is used for all shots. Learn it once and learn it right.

In speaking with Bobby Nichols, we asked him how to correctly grip a club, and he began by quoting his friend and former teacher, Henry Ranson, who called the perfect grip: "the palm and finger."

"By this I mean," explains Nichols, "start with the butt of the left hand, placing it at the heel of the club. Let the club run across the fingers and out through the very tip of your index finger on your left hand. In this position, the V formed by the left hand would then point almost to your right side." (Fig. 1., 2.)

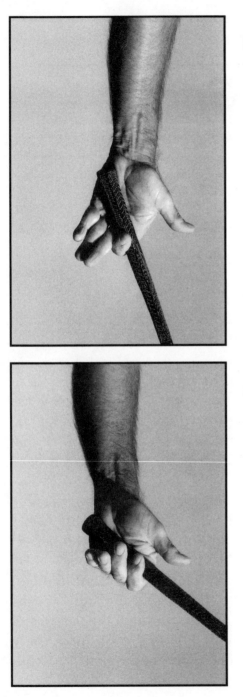

(Fig. 1.) The club rests on the second joint of the index finger, diagonally across palm and under fleshy pad of palm.

(Fig. 2.) The club is held in the fingers of the left hand.

This initial placement of the left hand on the club is the foundation for the entire grip, the linchpin of everyone's golf swing.

Having placed his left hand on the club, Nichols puts his left thumb to the left side of the shaft, (Fig. 3.) with the V of the hand pointed between his head and his right shoulder.

(Fig. 3.) *The left thumb is down the right side of the shaft.*

The right hand, according to Nichols, is used to refine the grip. "I use only a finger grip on my right hand. By that I mean I place the club only in my fingers." (Fig. 4.) The right-hand fingers are all that grip the club, and the two hands are linked together in what is called the Vardon overlapping grip. The little finger of the right hand overlaps the index finger of the left hand. (Fig. 5.) Nichols points out that putting the hands as close together as possible makes them work better. "They will get you maximum strength through the hitting area."

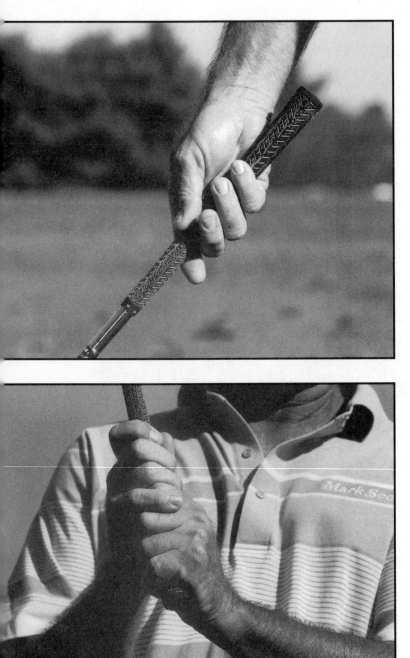

(Fig. 4.) The right hand is a finger grip as opposed to the palm grip of the left hand.

(Fig. 5.) The little finger of the right hand overlaps the left index finger.

The club should be gripped with all fingers, but they should not squeeze the shaft, nor should there be space between the hands or between the fingers. Both hands must work together. (Fig. 6.)

(Fig. 6.) *Both hands are tight together.*

Having established the correct position, both hands can then be adjusted to hook or slice the ball. If you move your left hand over the top of the club, in what is commonly called a "strong grip," your shoulders will be closed to the target.

By setting your hands in a weak position, with the right hand under the club, your right side will be dominant and the club face will be open at impact. But you can achieve a fade or a draw without complicating your swing by slightly moving your right or left hands.

"There are a lot of golf swings on the tour," Nichols adds, summing up. "I think Lee Trevino has about a half dozen himself. Even the great players, Sarazen or Hagan or anyone of their caliber, like Harry Cooper or Ben Hogan. They didn't swing the club the same way, yet they were great players. There is no one way to swing the golf club. But there is the right way to grip a club, and if you learn the basic technique, why, the game of golf will be nothing but child's play. I promise," he adds with a smile.

To get in the habit of gripping correctly, pick up the club with the left hand and grip the shaft as if you were making a left-handed handshake. Next, make a right-handed handshake and you'll have both hands properly on the club. If the shaft is firmly in the palm of the left hand and the fingers of the right, the Vs will work themselves into a correct position.

Once the grip is set, make sure it remains the same throughout the swing. To make sure that your hands aren't slipping—as Harry Cooper noticed Ben Hogan's were years ago—check the grip at the top of the swing, (Fig. 7.) and again when you've hit a ball. (Fig. 8.)

Any grip, because it is new, will feel uncomfortable, but stay with the correct form until the grip begins to feel natural, as it soon will.

(Fig. 7.) Crampton grips the club without tension, but holds tight at the top of the swing.

(Fig. 8.) *Hold the club tightly throughout the swing.*

Points to Remember

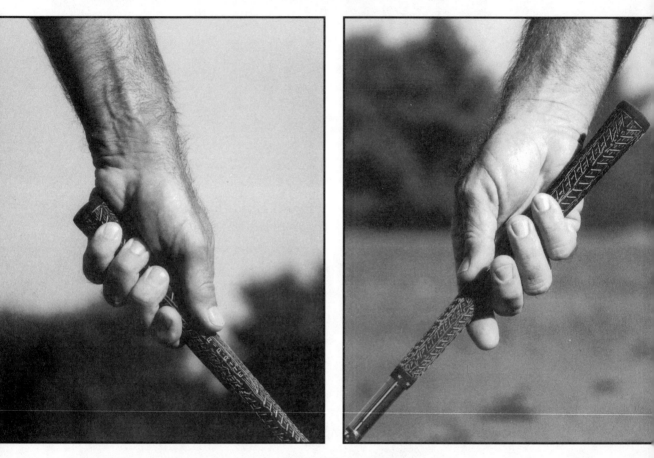

- *Place the left hand on the shaft first, with the thumb just over the center of the shaft.*

- *Bring the right hand lower onto the shaft and into contact with the left hand.*

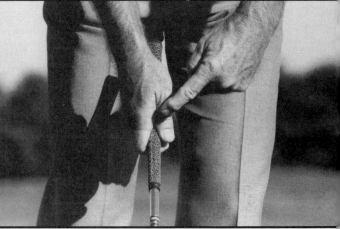

- The right thumb should lie across the center line of the club.

- The little finger of the right hand should overlap the left index finger beneath the shaft.

- The Vs formed by the thumb and forefinger of both hands should point to the right shoulder.

Playing with
the Correct Stance

The usual position taught beginning players is the square stance. By that we mean the shoulders, hips, and feet all are set square to the target.

To set yourself up in a square position, begin by aligning the left shoulder to the left of the pin, or to the left side of the fairway or target. As Harry Cooper points out in his introduction, most players position themselves to the right of the target.

You can remember to set the correct alignment by putting both of your feet together when you address the ball. Get the correct line and move your left foot first into position, then your right foot.

If you have any doubts about the alignment, set down a club in the same way your feet are positioned and check the line. (Fig. 1.)

The majority of the Senior Tour professionals think it is better to be slightly open at the setup as a way of getting the left side out of the way on the follow-through, especially with fairway woods and longer irons.

(Fig. 1.) Casper uses a club to check his set up.

Play the ball off the heel of your left foot. And position the ball far enough out in front of you so that you can reach for it comfortably with the club. Don't stretch, or let the ball position squeeze you and force you to bend your left arm. (Fig. 2.)

Your feet are spread apart about the same width as your shoulders, with the weight of your body balanced between both feet and distributed evenly from the toes to the heels. Both feet are toed outward.

In such a square stance, your left shoulder, arm, and hand will naturally rise, and the right side will drop. (Fig. 3.)

You're now set to hit the ball.

(Fig. 2.) Crampton is not reaching for the ball.

(Fig. 3.) Crampton's right shoulder is lower than his left at the setup.

Points to Remember

- Position the left shoulder to the left of the target.

- Place the ball off the left heel.

- Open the stance slightly by dropping back the left foot.

- Reach, don't stretch, for the ball.

BRUCE CRAMPTON

BIRTHDATE: September 28, 1935

BIRTHPLACE: Sydney, Australia

RESIDENCE: Dallas, Texas

JOINED PGA TOUR: 1957

PGA TOUR VICTORIES: 15

PGA TOUR CAREER EARNINGS: $1,374,294

JOINED SENIOR PGA TOUR: 1985

SENIOR TOUR VICTORIES THROUGH 1989: 15

SENIOR TOUR EARNINGS THROUGH 1989: $1,239,380

CAREER EARNINGS: $2,615,573

BEST YEAR ON SENIOR PGA TOUR: $454,299 (1986)

BRUCE CRAMPTON

Golf's Iron Man

For Bruce Crampton, the Senior Tour came along at a time in his life when he was secure in his golf game as well as secure in his life. He didn't feel that his profession was a struggle. "When I was playing on the regular tour, I often felt that I was just getting by from one year to the next."

What made it easier for Crampton is that the field is smaller on the Senior Tour and there are no cuts after thirty-six holes. The Senior Tour also provides courtesy cars, which means Bruce is able to fly between tournaments, and the increase in prize money means he can not only afford to pay his caddie more, but also keep the same caddie from event to event. Because the Senior Tour players are treated so well, "We simply play better," Crampton sums up.

Today for senior players like himself, "Everything really is bigger, better, and we all appreciate the benefits."

Crampton came onto the Senior Tour after a brilliant professional career on the PGA Tour. He first turned professional in 1953 back home in Sydney, Australia, and won the Australian Open in 1956, when he was only twenty. He then moved to America and won the Milwaukee Open in 1961, edging out Gay Brewer and Bob Goalby. His finest year on tour was in 1973, when he won four times and finished second in five other events. Twice the winner of the Vardon Trophy, he also was the fifth tour millionaire and the first non-American to win over $200,000 in a single year.

In 1977 he retired from the tour to spend his time developing oil and gas wells in Texas, his adopted state.

It was during this layoff from the tour that he began to study his golf swing. "It gave me the opportunity to look at old films of my game and videotapes of tournaments that I won. I read articles about my playing, read some criticism as well, and some of the better players—golfers like Byron Nelson, for one—made comments about my golf swing that were very helpful. I had the opportunity to sit back and review my career without having to go through the ordeal of trying to play tournament golf everyday.

"I think that period of reflection prepared me for the Senior Tour. It gave me a greater understanding of my golf swing. Today, I'm hitting the ball better. I trust my golf swing more. And I think the fundamentals of my swing are a lot better than they were when I was on the regular tour."

Since joining the Senior Tour in 1985, Crampton has won fifteen times, including a run of seven victories in 1986, when he was named Senior Tour Player-of-the-Year. In 1989, he won two tournaments and over $450,000, finishing sixth in the official Senior PGA Tour money list.

What has also helped Bruce is his physical fitness. Bruce exercises aerobically while on the tour, and this has given him a sense of well-being and a good feeling about his body. "I think it's all incorporated. I don't think there's any one thing, but it's just a combination of a whole lot of things."

A major influence on Crampton's well-being and his successful golf career in the Senior Tour has been his involvement with sports psychologists. He has listened to tapes by Barbara Taylor and Dr. Koops, and worked with Bill Mitchell and his mental-dynamics techniques, which involve the subconscious and subliminal responses.

"I think I'm better equipped to play up to the potential that I'm capable of playing, more so than I've ever been in the past."

Unlike many of the other Senior Tour players who are allowed to use carts, Bruce walks the whole round. "I walk because otherwise I get to the next shot too quickly. I am used to walking, and I have more time to think."

But there are problems with his walking between shots. "We're required to play quicker on this tour than the other tour. We have only forty seconds to make a shot, not the forty-five seconds that is allowed on the PGA Tour. Our 'slow play' rule is more stringent than theirs.

"There is also a problem when we play in the pro-am. I'm walking and they are riding in carts. It seems then that the only time we get to talk is on the green or tee. So in many respects, I'm not for having carts used at our events."

Unlike many other professionals, Crampton is not involved with golf course construction. "Right now," he says, "I'm still trying to play on these golf courses, not design them."

Crampton is a fan, however, of many of the new courses being designed by men like Peter Dye. "I'm also very partial to Pete Guy's work. I really admire his creativity and originality. I think the man's a genius. I don't believe in pampering myself and I don't want to be pampered on the golf course. I find that Pete Guy's work challenges me.

There's other good players who have built courses. I think Jack Nicklaus has does a very fine job.

"But I really love the old architecture. I had the opportunity to play Pine Valley recently, and it is undoubtedly the best natural golf course in the world. I don't know whether it's the best. For me, I like the layout at the PGA West Stadium course because there's 18 great holes. They're difficult and they're demanding.

"However, now they're getting all the condominiums and the town houses built around the layout, and it's kind of changing its flavor. The layout is still the same, but just the overall feeling of the golf course out there has changed. And when you play somewhere like Pine Valley and you realize that these courses were built in the days when they didn't have earth-moving equipment, you've really got to admire what they did. Pine Valley is a masterpiece.

"But if I had to pick a golf course to be around the rest of my life, just for sheer pleasure and enjoyment, I think I'd pick Cypress Point on the Monterey Peninsula. To me it's like five or six different types of golf courses all in one. You go from parkland on the first few holes into the British Open type of environment for the next couple of holes, then you get in dense pine trees, and come out onto the sand dunes and back to a British Open-type course. The finishing holes—15, 16, and 17— are right along the ocean, a totally different look. And the final hole is something else entirely, because it's in those eerie cypress trees with the red moss on them."

Bruce Crampton plans to play on the Senior Tour as long as he can. "We've got the over sixty—Super Seniors—to look forward to. I'm anxious to see what happens when I get to be sixty along with Billy Casper and Miller Barber and Don January." (Fig. 1.)

The combinations of professional PGA tours make it

(Fig. 1.) *Bruce Crampton still playing championship golf in the lengthening twilight of his career.*

possible for Crampton and others to play golf all their life. And Crampton sees the game of golf much like life itself.

"You play a great round of golf and you think you've got the game by the tail. You make a birdie, but then turn around and make a double bogey on the very next hole. You think you've hit a good shot and you end up in a divot hole. Now, life's like that. You can't look into the future and anticipate what's going to happen on the golf course, you just got to do the best you can with what you've got to work with. It's one shot at a time. Life is the same way. One day at a time."

Crampton is not very emotional on the golf course, but he does "dwell more on the good shots," as he says, and takes "nourishment from them," while the fans and the press will tend to remember and talk about all of the bad shots he made.

"I live on the great two-on shot that I hit at Phoenix this year or Indianapolis and some of the other great shots I've hit. I remember what it feels like to win so that I can recall that when needed and keep reminding myself that I'm still capable of winning every time I play."

Playing off
the Tee

The key to any shot in golf is being comfortable over the ball. This is particularly true with the driver—the longest club in the bag, and for many, the most difficult club to hit.

If you can manage to get off the tee with some distance, however, it gives you a better chance at scoring. The task then is to make your driver work for you.

Before driving, take a moment to study the shot, to see what the hole looks like, and, more important, to visualize how your ball will travel off the tee and into position for your next shot. (Fig. 1.)

Bruce Crampton is a great believer in the power of positive thinking. He tells the story of when he was still in short pants back in Australia and dreaming of playing golf on the American tour. "I must have been thirteen years old and I was watching the American players when they came out to play, dreaming and fantasizing about coming to the United States. When I played, I'd say things like, 'I've got to knock this six-iron close to win a tournament.' Even at that age I was getting my subconscious ready to find a way to do it."

(Fig. 1.) Crampton sees where he's playing.

Crampton uses this same psychological approach to playing a shot on the golf course, explaining it this way, "How many times have you got water on the left or out-of-bounds, you say don't hit it left and that's exactly what you do! Or you've got a bad lie. And you're thinking, I don't know whether I can get this in the air, or whatever.

"You've got to get into a can-do frame of mind. And you'll find that most successful people do that. Anyone who has made a success of their life will identify with what I'm saying. The game is just played in a different arena, with the same principles. You have to have great self-discipline, work lots of hours, and make sacrifices to be successful at the game."

The way you stand at the ball on the tee is the same basic setup for any golf shot. The weight is between the balls and heels of your feet. The knees are slightly flexed. Most professionals will drop their left leg back and away from the line a few inches and also turn out the left toe, so that their body is in an open position, allowing them to be able to shift their weight and move through the shot.

Crampton believes one should stand erect for this shot. "I think that golf should be played in an erect position. Not only mechanics-wise is that good, but I think physically it's good. When players have poor posture and bend over too much at address, it tends to put the task of making of the golf stroke on the lower back instead of on the legs. I don't think that one would walk down the fairway in a bent-over, hunched position, nor should they hit the golf ball that way." (Fig. 2.)

Once set up, you must remember to swing within yourself. For Crampton this means not trying to overpower the driver. "I try to keep a smooth tempo and make a good, solid contact with the ball."

Playing within himself, Crampton finds he hits the ball

(Fig. 2.) *Stand erect at the address.*

farther. "This is hard to do," he admits, "because the more
solid you hit it, the more ego comes into it and the harder
you want to beat it on the next drive because you want to
really make it fly down the fairway."

Crampton sets up in an open position so that he can
drive through the shot with his legs and have his left hip
clear on the way down. (Fig. 3.)

(Fig. 3.) Crampton moves his left knee out of the way.

He begins the backswing by taking the club, his hands and his shoulders away from the ball, in one smooth motion and as one piece. (Fig. 4.)

As Crampton points out, if the club, arms, and shoulders aren't moving together off the ball, the shot must be rearranged someplace else in the swing.

(Fig. 4.) *Move the club back in one motion.*

He keeps the club going back as long as possible before he breaks his wrists, since cocking the wrist this early will likely means that the right hand becomes involved with the swing, and he'll most likely "hit from the top" of the swing and lose all power. (Fig. 5.)

(Fig. 5.) *Break the wrists at the last possible moment.*

The tendency on a big swing is always to sway off the ball, and Crampton prevents that by keeping the weight of his body on the inside edge of his right foot during the backswing.

He also maintains this balance by moving his left knee inward as he turns. (Figure 6.) His left shoulder has moved under his chin by the time he has reached the top of his swing.

Coming down, his left side is again leading the way. He

(Fig. 6.) *Left knee moves inward.*

pulls the club back and through the ball, making sure that he doesn't break his wrists until they are below his waistline.

Most important in Crampton's swing is his ability to keep his wrists uncocked until the last moment. "The longer I can keep my wrists delayed on the way down, the farther I'm going to hit the ball and the more I'm going to be underneath it or behind it and less over the top of it." (Fig. 7.)

(Fig. 7.) *Hit underneath the ball.*

At impact, Crampton is behind the ball. This position allows his shoulders to get under the shot (Fig. 8.) while his legs drive through. His head is steady and behind the ball. His left hand and his left arm are square and straight and face the target. (Fig. 9.)

The swing finishes on its own centrifugal force. The club face is carried up and around. Crampton is also a

(Fig. 8.) *Crampton is still behind the ball at impact.*

great believer in striking the ball with the major muscles of the body—the upper arm and back muscles. His rationale is that when a player swings with his hands and smaller muscles of the forearms and wrists, the large muscles can't keep up. "They are always going to be uncoordinated and out of sync. However, if you think more about your major muscles, your little muscles can always keep up."

(Fig. 9.) *His stance is square to the target after impact.*

A golfer should concentrate on making a bigger turn, which in turn will mean a better golf swing. "Try to think just about swinging the club," Crampton sums up, "and just letting the ball get in the way."

He also makes the point that golf is really a left-arm game, and right-handed players are at a disadvantage. "We've spent our lives," says Bruce, "hammering nails with our right hand, playing baseball, playing tennis, and hitting at it with our right hand, playing baseball, playing

(Fig. 10.) Crampton stops at midpoint in his backswing.

tennis, and hitting at it with our right hand, but golf is played from the opposite side. I have to play with my left side, my left arm, the upper part of my left arm.''

Crampton uses a small exercise to get into the right position for his drive. He gets square to his target, takes the club back so far, (Fig. 10.) and feels what it is like at that position. Next he takes the club to the top of the swing, where it is parallel to the ground, (Fig. 11.) and sees how his body has turned on the swing.

(Fig. 11.) *Checks the swing at the top of the backswing.*

Bringing the club back, he notes the position where the left arm is underneath, again getting the feel of the position of his hands, arms, and the club. (Fig. 12.) He notes where the cocking of the wrists takes place so he understands how dominant his left arm is, and how the right hand doesn't play much of a role in the swing and at impact. (Fig. 13.)

(Fig. 12.) *Finds the correct position on the downswing.*

(Fig. 13.) *Sets himself at the correct position at impact.*

"What happens is that your brain learns to fire the muscles in the correct order in your subconscious, in your memory banks. You can create this feeling. A lot of people don't know what it feels like to be in the correct position at the top. This will help them if they do it correctly. It will place them in the correct position and they'll know what it feels like to be in the correct hitting position at the top, through the swing, and in the follow-through."

Points to Remember

• *Be comfortable over the ball.*

• *Drop the left foot off the line.*

• *Take the club back in one motion.*

- *Break the wrists on the down-swing at the last possible moment.*

  - *Stay behind the ball at impact.*

Playing the Mid-irons

Everyone who plays golf loves to hit the mid-irons. They are the easiest clubs in the bag to play. The problem is hitting the ball close to the pin. And that can be a real problem, especially on difficult, sloping greens.

A golfer must first decide on the distance to the green, and then on what club is necessary.

The most common mistake that middle- and high-handicap players make with the mid-iron is misjudging the distance. When a player is not sure of the distance, there is always a tendency to force the shot.

If you are playing a course that you know, then calculating the distance is less of a problem. Over time you'll come to know what club is needed from almost any position, on and off the fairway.

You have to trust your own swing, to know that a five-iron is right for you even if your playing partner reaches for a six-iron. So, get the distance in mind and visualize the shot, knowing that you have the right club in your hands for this distance. (Fig. 1.)

(Fig. 1.) *Take a moment to see the shot.*

Remember, too, that when you are playing on a new course, the distance will always seem shorter. If in doubt, take the longer iron, don't force the shot, and just swing within yourself, as the professionals say.

All professionals on the Senior Tour know the exact yardage from a half-dozen points on a fairway. They and their caddies have already "walked" the course, charting distance from water heads and bushes. For the player at home, there is often a marker at 150 yards to give everyone a ready gauge of the distance to the green.

Having decided on the distance, and more important, the exact distance to where the pin is cut, the next decision is what mid-iron to play.

The mid-irons are the clubs we hit most off on the fairway. In an average round of golf, we hit the four-, five-, and six-irons at least ten times. Hitting these clubs so often gives anyone a chance to score, to get the ball close to the pin for a par or a possible birdie. No one can score well unless he can hit the mid-irons.

Fortunately, the mid-irons, most likely the five-iron, is the club that most players first hit well. Many players go back to the five-iron when something goes wrong with their swing. The club is not too long or too heavy. So if your swing begins to cause you trouble, cure it by returning to your favorite mid-iron.

One reason that the mid-irons are "easier" to hit is because of the length of the shaft and the loft of the club. There actually isn't a standard set in the rules of golf, but most golf-club manufacturers have their own standard of thirty-two degrees for a five-iron, with a four change (either higher or lower) for all the other irons.

The longer irons (two-, three-, four-) have less loft, and the ball therefore will have a lower trajectory, much more roll, and achieve greater distance. The shorter irons (seven-, eight-, nine-) have more loft, higher trajectory, and give the player the ability to create backswing and hold the ball on a smooth green.

Bruce demonstrated for us how to play the mid-irons. Apart from the basic fundamentals of grip, according to him, the posture and setup are the next most important aspects of the swing.

"It's imperative with any iron that the hands are slightly ahead of the ball so that on the downswing the club will hit the ball first, then turf. (Fig. 2.) This pinches the ball between the club facing the turf and of course imparts the necessary back spin." (Fig. 3.)

(Fig. 2.) *Crampton places his hands ahead of the shot at the address.*

(Fig. 3.) *Breaks the hands at the last possible moment, pinching the ball between the club and turf.*

Crampton, like most professionals, plays the ball off the left instep regardless of what iron he has in his hands. Playing the ball from this position, he sets up left of the target so as to work the ball from left to right. He has found that if he plays the ball back farther in his stance, he will hit the ball harder, and by playing it forward, he will achieve a softer, easier swing.

For the mid-iron, Crampton stands in an erect position with a slightly open stance, much more open than a wood because he wants to be able to clear his left side to allow the left arm to carry the club along the intended line of flight. The left arm acts as a leader.

"When I was younger I used to practice by just hitting shorter shots with just my left arm on the club. I've found in any golf shot—and this is particularly true with this iron—that whenever I play it with my hands, I'm the most inaccurate." This iron shot should be played with the major muscles, with the hands just along for the ride. Crampton therefore plays the shot with the upper part of his left arm. He attempts to get his hands as high in the backswing as he possibly can, making sure that he turns the shoulders sufficiently in the backswing, and completes the swing with a high follow-through so as not to come over the shot when he finishes. "When I finish I'm watching the ball from underneath." (Fig. 4., 5., 6., 7.)

Crampton has found that many golfers get very quick with their swing because they are insecure on the shorter shots. "They're trying to help the ball in the air."

For him the key to slowing down the golf swing is to think about accelerating through the shot. "Basically, what I mean is to begin the gradual acceleration from the top."

In order to accelerate, one must slow the club down at the top. Bruce believes that psychologically it's much easier to accomplish this when the player is thinking about accelerating through the shot rather than trying to slow the swing down, or slow the backswing down, or be slow at the top.

"What I'm attempting to do with the shot is hit it high and soft. I want to carry it in the vicinity of the flag, expecting it to stop. Therefore, I start the ball to the left of the flag and let it gradually fall toward the target, which is the softest flight so that it will stop more rapidly."

What Crampton is describing is the basic setup—with the hands high on the backswing and follow-through—for a straightforward shot when the player has normal green conditions and normal pin placement, as well as a good lie. Such a shot depends on the lie, of course. It cannot be done from rough or long grass, where the ball will tend to fly on the player. This normal shot also changes with a downhill, side-hill, or uphill lie. Then the player has to "recreate" another shot for that situation. But for most players, if they learn how to hit the mid-iron safely from the fairway, then that is one shot they can depend on and feel good about. It is also a shot that commonly comes into play in a round of golf.

(Fig. 4.–7.) Crampton's beautiful swing, start to finish. Note the three-quarter backswing, the complete turn, and the late release of his wrists.

Points to Remember

* *Know the distance.*   * *Stand erect at the ball.*

- *Play the mid-irons off the left heel.*

  - *Hands forward with the left hand leading the shot.*

    - *Swing smoothly.*

BILLY CASPER

BIRTHDATE: June 24, 1931

BIRTHPLACE: San Diego, California

RESIDENCE: Chula Vista, California

JOINED PGA TOUR: 1955

PGA TOUR VICTORIES: 51

SENIOR TOUR VICTORIES THROUGH 1989: 9

SENIOR TOUR EARNINGS THROUGH 1989: $1,086,068

CAREER EARNINGS: $2,774,726

BEST YEAR ON SENIOR PGA TOUR: $211,698 (1987)

BILLY CASPER
Golf's Quiet Man

During the 1960s, in the era of the "Big Three"—Arnold Palmer, Gary Player, and Jack Nicklaus—there was another great golfer who lived in their shadow and played his own brand of steady, winning golf. His name was Billy Casper, and to many he is one of the finest golfers to play the game.

Between the years 1956 and 1975, Casper won fifty-one tournaments, led the PGA in money earnings twice, collected five Vardon Trophies for low scoring average, and was twice the PGA Player-of-the-Year. Casper also won two U.S. Opens and the 1970 Masters.

Billy Casper has never been a flamboyant player. He did not have Palmer's charisma, or Nicklaus's power, but he did know how to win golf tournaments. He won in 1956, his first year on tour, and he won a tournament every year after that through 1971. Not many players—not even Palmer or Nicklaus—can make that claim. For fifteen straight years he was always in the winner's circle.

And it was not easy for Billy Casper. From the beginning of his professional career, he endured continual problems with his weight. Golf is a slim man's game and Casper was anything but slim. In 1959 when he won the U.S. Open at Winged Foot (a year in which he won five tournaments) he weighed over 212 pounds.

Casper attempted to lose weight in those years, but he never could. It wasn't until a Chicago physician finally discovered that he was allergic to a variety of common foods that he was able to develop a special diet—which included swordfish, buffalo meat and avocado pears— enabling him to lose weight and continue to play winning golf.

His greatest years in golf followed this loss of weight. In 1965 he lost over forty pounds and won four tournaments, and by 1968 he virtually dominated the PGA Tour, winning six tournaments that year and over $200,000.

Casper is perhaps best remembered on the PGA Tour for what happened to him in the 1966 U.S. Open held at the Olympic Club in San Francisco. He was trailing Arnold Palmer by seven shots on the final day with nine holes to play when Palmer faltered, and Casper, playing brilliantly, tied him and forced a next day playoff. Again, Palmer led early, but Casper closed quickly and beat Palmer by six shots.

In early 1972, Casper's game began to slip, and his interest in playing tournament golf faded with his poor play. A deeply religious man, and father of nine children (six of them adopted), Billy returned to his home in San Diego and concentrated on the development of his golf camps for kids, which he has operated for over seventeen years.

But then came the Senior Tour in 1980 and a second chance for him as a professional touring pro. (Fig. 1.)

Like many other golfers from the 1960s "golden age" of

(Fig. 1.) Billy Casper is in his second great career playing
on the Seniors PGA Tour.

golf, Casper had reached the age of forty thinking he'd never play competitively again. The Senior Tour meant there was a new tour for the likes of him, but Casper wasn't ready for the match.

"Even before the Senior Tour came along," recalls Casper, "I had no confidence in my game. My swing had simply deteriorated. I started to work with Phil Rogers, the great golf instructor.

"I changed my grip, my swing, and I also used hypnosis, working with a woman trained in self-hypnosis. I worked with her because I knew it was a psychological problem that I was experiencing as well as a physical problem.

"Eventually I got to a man that worked with athletes in hypnosis and he helped me tremendously. What we did was to take the film of my 1966 U.S. Open win, the film of my 1970 Master's win, all the positive things that happened: my good shots, good putts, good swings. He spliced them together and made about a twelve-minute tape and I'd watch it both under hypnosis and out of hypnosis, trying to appeal to the subconscious that I could do these things again. I was trying to prove to myself that I could still play golf."

Still, with all of this work and help, Casper's swing and game did not improve.

"I finally got to the point with Phil Rogers that I told him I thought I was wasting his time," Casper remembers. "I was hitting one good shot out of every twenty-five balls I hit. And then when I hit a shot that I thought was pretty good, Phil would say that it was a piece of garbage. It took me nearly five years to rebuild my swing."

Casper came back to winning golf by changing his swing.

"I've always believed that you took the club straight back as far as you could, and then you broke your wrist to a point where you were parallel at the top of the swing. I had a great lateral movement of my hips and that created a blocking sensation because I also had a very strong grip.

"However, I moved my hips well and this allowed me to keep the blade of the club square at impact. But as I got older I couldn't move as well. I just wasn't as supple. I had days when I was hitting the ball a hundred-fifty, two hundred yards off line. I never knew where the ball might go.

"I was discouraged and embarrassed to be out there playing golf. I went from a scoring average of under 70 to one around 78. Then the Senior Tour came along. Seeing a second chance, I went to work with Phil, used self-hypnosis, and I changed my swing to fit a man of fifty. It took me five years, but I was ready when it was my turn to join the tour."

He joined the tour in Massachusetts and finished in a tie for seventh. It took him only a year to win, and he won twice in 1981. From that point on, it has been ever higher. Last year on the tour he earned over $198,000.

Playing the
Fairway Wood

As important as visualizing the drive is, it is much more important to "see" the fairway wood shot. This long shot, which often involves potential trouble, is the one that puts the player into a position to make a birdie, or at least save a par.

Approach the fairway wood shot from behind, seeing what lies ahead in the way of bunkers, out-of-bounds, and other possible hazards. The first decision a player makes is whether he can reach the green with the fairway wood, and if not, where he wants to place the ball for the next shot to the green.

In making his decision where to aim, for example, Billy Casper always finds a target. "If I were hitting a shot toward a pine tree, I'd set up just to the right of it and then work the ball toward the target."

As many of the professionals on tour have said, you have to begin by trusting in your swing, and by not letting your subconscious decide that however you play the ball, it will end up in trouble. Understanding where you want the ball to land goes a long way toward being successful with any shot. Golf is a game of confidence.

With the fairway wood, golfers have as their advantage the fact that the fairway wood is one of the easier clubs to hit, certainly easier to hit than a long iron. Many of the professionals on the Senior Tour carry an extra wood, either a five- or six-wood, and pull the two- and three-irons out of their bags entirely.

For the average golfer, the fairway wood is a better choice of club. The swing is a much more sweeping action, and the club head comes into the ball at a lower angle than that of a iron. Also, the wood provides more of a hitting area and with a normal swing, the ball will react better. One can actually miss a four-wood and still get distance from the shot for the mere reason that the wood provides more mass. This is very important when playing out of the rough, since most golfers aren't strong enough to get a long iron through the grass. Also, for a really good player a four-wood will carry between 220 and 240 yards, much farther than a one- or two-iron.

The three-, four-, and even five-woods are played basically the same way. Billy Casper, for example, moves the ball just off his left heel. "What I'm trying to do is catch the ball at the bottom of the swing and sweep it up. I don't hit down, nor do I hit up on the ball. I catch it right at the bottom of the swing." (Fig. 1.)

In setting up for the fairway wood, place your right foot in position first, then place the left foot. Getting set this way, you'll ensure yourself of getting the correct direction to the target. When hitting into a tight green, especially one that is well bunkered, the setup and direction are very

What a player has to remember is that the fairway wood can't be forced. Casper, for one, always hits the ball soft. And, like Bruce Crampton, he plays within himself. He

(Fig. 1.) Casper, moving through the ball, catches it at the bottom of his swing.

doesn't try to "make something happen" with a spectacular shot. He knows that the odds are always against him.

"If you try to make that great shot and hit the ball hard," Billy points out, "you'll get your shoulder going under, and that's when you'll pull it. Or your head will get behind the ball as you swing. Always remember that if the ball starts off your target line, you'll never draw it back in."

Billy takes a wide stance, which does limit his swing, and he draws the fairway wood back very low to the ground and without breaking his wrist. The first "cocking" of the club occurs when he is above waist high. He then lets his hands and arms work naturally, never forcing the action or rushing the downswing. His swing is short and smooth, and he does not "make up" for the shortness with a sudden, jerky power return to the point of impact. Casper is a gentle, soft-spoken man, and he swings the same way. Or as he likes to put it, "never too long, never too short." (Fig. 2., 3., 4., 5., 6.)

Casper has always used a three-quarter swing. (Fig. 9.) "Distance to the green frightens people," Casper believes, "and so they think they have to power the ball. What you should remember is that if you take half a swing, you're cutting down your chances of making a mistake."

What Billy might lack in power and sheer physical ability at his age is compensated for with the new golf equipment that is on the market.

Metal woods are one example of a club that has helped these senior pros, as well as more amateur golfers. Casper, like almost all of those on the Senior Tour, uses metal woods. For Billy it is an easier club to control and one that is "very forgiving when you make a bad swing."

Finding the special advantage, of course, has always been central to Casper's success. He never had the great

FIG. 2.   FIG. 3.

physical strength of Palmer or Nicklaus. He did not have
the great shot-making skills of a player like Seve Ballesteros.
Rather, he has always been a great putter and someone
who knew how to "manage" a round of golf.

"For me, half of the game is deciding what to do with
each shot. I put a premium on knowing where I want to

FIG. 4.

FIG. 5.

(Fig. 2., 3.) *Casper's short swing takes the club head only three-quarters of the way back.*

(Fig. 4., 5.) *On the downswing he moves his left side out of the way.*

play the ball so that I'll have the right position. I play each shot so that the next one will be easier for me."

Golf played that way is very much like playing billiards. A good billiards player continually positions the cue ball for the next shot. Learning this skill of managing one's game is perhaps harder than learning how to hit a dead-

(Fig. 6.) *On his follow-through he finishes high.*

solid perfect golf shot. Certainly, "golf management" comes with experience, with the number of rounds played, but according to Casper, there are basic principles that can be quickly mastered by anyone.

And they are simply:

• Always play the percentage shot, the safe shot.
• Don't rush the shot.
• Know what you're capable of doing with your swing.

Naturally, playing the ball off the fairway requires another consideration, and that is the lie. Make sure before you play that you can get the face of a wood behind the ball. If the lie is tight, however, you don't have to abandon the wood; go instead to one with more loft. Remember, you will not need as much club on a tight lie because more grass will come between the wood and the ball, causing the ball to fly. You'll pick up the extra yards you've lost changing clubs. However, if the ball is sitting up, you have to be sure that you don't hit through the ball, missing it.

A wood also allows you to work the ball into the green or around hazards. To fade the ball, simply move the left foot off the line and turn the left toe out a few degrees. This will help you make the turn.

For the hook, or draw, shot, close the stance slightly and play the ball off the toe of the left foot. The ball will run farther with a hook shot, and that must be taken into consideration when judging distance.

Points to Remember

- Move the ball to a position off the left heel.
    - Use a three-quarter swing.
        - Don't rush the shot.

- *Strike the ball at the bottom of the swing and sweep it off the grass.*

- *Place the right foot in position first, then place the left.*

Playing the
Long Iron

Most golfers agree that the long iron is the most difficult club in the bag to hit. It is a club with an awkward length and a tiny face. It also requires a good mental attitude by a player just to make a good swing.

For the professional, the long iron is one club that they must hit well. Playing on long, competitive courses, they often have a second shot into the green that requires a two- or three-iron. They also need to be accurate, since the greens are often small or tucked behind a bunker. They have to hit a three-iron 210 yards and they have to be on target.

The majority of professionals, especially young ones, will hit down on a long iron, driving the ball toward the green—"banging" the ball—whereas with a shorter club, they will hit a high, floating shot.

Billy Casper, and other professionals on the Senior Tour, suggest that the amateur player forget how the long iron is played by PGA pros. They advise instead that middle- and high-handicap players hit the long iron their way.

To explain how this is done, Billy Casper demonstrates with a three-iron.

"I believe all irons should be played two to three inches in back of the left heel, with the weight evenly distributed on both feet. (Fig. 1.)

"I close my stance slightly because I like to line up to the right of my target and draw the ball from the right to the left." (Fig. 2.)

(Fig. 1.) *Play the ball three inches off left heel.*
(Fig. 2.) *Left foot slightly forward in stance.*

When Casper was younger, he did attempt to play with a fade, as a way of controlling his shots, but for most of his life he has naturally drawn the ball from right to left, which has allowed him to achieve distance off the tee.

"At the setup, I also place my hands in back of the ball. If you start from this position when you swing, then you'll get back to the same position when you make contact with the ball. But if you start with your hands too far forward when you swing, then you'll be off the ball when you return to impact. That's a very important point to remember. (Fig. 3.)

(Fig. 3.) *Hands are behind the ball at the address.*

FIG. 4.

"What's also important to remember is the basic setup. At my golf camp for children, I make sure that my instructors teach two basic fundamentals. One is the grip—because that is the only contact the body has with the club and the ball. The second is the alignment. If you pay attention to just these two basics of the game, you will become a good golfer."

Today Casper swings the club back on the inside, gets it into position, and then brings it down on the inside. He works underneath the ball and picks it off the grass rather than beating down the ball. (Fig. 4., 5., 6., 7.)

FIG. 5.   FIG. 6.   FIG. 7.

(Fig. 4.–7.) Keep the club on the inside throughout the swing.

To understand how this will work for your swing, practice hitting the iron and seeing where your body is positioned. At the top of the swing, just before starting the downswing, your left shoulder should be under your chin, and your right shoulder higher than the left. Your weight should have shifted to the inside of your right foot, but your hips have barely shifted at all. (Fig. 8.)

On the downswing, your left knee will kick out to open

(Fig. 8.) *Hold the weight on the inside of your body.*

up your left side, and your head and shoulders stay behind the shot so as to give it power. (Fig. 9.)

Starting down, your speed picks up and your left hand pulls the club down and forward. With a slightly open stance, with your pivot working, you come into the point of impact with the freedom to drive the ball.

Finishing the shot isn't a problem, since the centrifugal force of the swing will bring you through with a transfer of

(Fig. 9.) *Keep behind the ball at impact.*

weight to the left side and a high finish. When you finish this way, you know you have hit a fine shot. (Fig. 10.)

"If I want to fade the ball," Casper explains, "I open my stance. And when I do that, my shoulders, hips, and feet are all pointing to the left.

"Also, to help the fade, I open the blade. When I swing, I swing down across from the outside and this spins the ball to the right. So I aim left, swing left, and the ball goes right. A tricky game, isn't it?" he says, smiling.

(Fig. 10.) *Finish high.*

All his life, Casper has been known as a player who "plays" within himself. In the age of the great power hitters—Palmer, Nicklaus, and Player—Casper never extended himself. He has said that he never really used more than eighty-five percent of his muscular capability.

Casper does not "bang" the ball as much as he works it toward the target, using his strong grip, his natural hook, and his ability to move his left hip out of the way during the downswing, clearing his body away from the ball so that his wrists won't roll over prematurely and cause a dangerous duck hook.

Casper has a very natural and smooth swing. Watching the way that he stays within himself, gathering his swing together at the top of the downswing and then accelerating the club head toward the point of impact, one can easily understand why he still is a great player. (Fig. 11., 12., 13., 14., 15., 16., 17., 18., 19.)

FIG. 11.

FIG. 12.

FIG. 13.

FIG. 14.

(Fig. 11.-14.) On the backswing move the club back on the inside to the top of a three-quarters swing.

FIG. 15.

FIG. 16.

FIG. 17.

FIG. 18.   FIG. 19.

(Fig. 15.–19.) *Casper stays within himself on every shot, working only with a three-quarter swing.*

Points to Remember

- *The iron should be played two or three inches in back of the left heel.*

  - *At the setup, position the hands back of the ball.*

    - *The shoulders, hips, and feet have to be on the same line.*

- Take the club back on the inside and bring it down on the inside.

- Work underneath the ball and pick it off the grass.

- Hit the ball softly.

BOB WATSON

BIRTHDATE: July 10, 1923
BIRTHPLACE: Wichita Falls, Texas
RESIDENCE: Jupiter Inlet Colony, Florida
JOINED PGA: 1950
TOURNAMENT VICTORIES: 8
CLUB AFFILIATION: Westchester Country Club
PROFESSIONAL HONORS:
  President of Metropolitan Professional
    Golfers Association, 3 terms
  Metropolitan PGA Golf Professional of the
    Year, 1972
  Metropolitan PGA Hall of Fame, 1986

BOB WATSON
Home Professional

Bob Watson came out of West Texas in the early Fifties at a time when the PGA Tour was very small. The majority of players worked as home professionals in the northern states during the summer months, then played throughout the South in winter. They also played in what was once called the Caribbean Tour.

Watson did play in the South and on the Caribbean Tour. (He won the Panama Open in 1958, where he beat seven of the ten leading money winners of that year, and the Colombian Open in 1960.) But having married young and needing a steady income, he has spent the majority of his time as a home professional in New York state.

This year, after fifteen years as the golf director at the Westchester Country Club, Watson retired to Florida, where he plans to play full-time in Jupiter Inlet Colony.

In Florida he plays with, as he puts it, "the older pros," who are still out on the practice range driving balls.

"We're all still trying to keep swinging. Our main goal is to turn, turn, turn—keep making full turns on our swings.

(Fig. 1.) Bob Watson uses the long putter to keep in the game.

That's the secret for driving a ball! We want that full swing, but as we get older, we get tighter, and so we're using graphite shafts, longer clubs, new high-test balls, anything at all to gain a few extra yards off the tee."

Watson also recently switched over to the long putter because as he got older he began to develop the "yips." He admits that he never was a great putter, but now, "just before contact, I'd tend to 'yip' it with my right hand. I switched to the long putter, and I find that as a tall person I'm much more comfortable over the ball. I'm also finding that I'm putting better, which is a pleasant surprise."

While at the Westchester Country Club, Bob Watson played three or four times a week with members, and also played competitively on the New York Senior Tour. He has twice been the Metropolitan PGA Seniors Champion.

After a lifetime of golf, Watson, at age sixty-seven, is also still trying to swing long and loose. "It's harder," he admits, "but I like to hear the guys on the practice tee ask me, 'Bobby, how do you get the club way back?'

"Remarks like that keep me playing. That and a few good shots and sinking a few long putts." (Fig. 1.)

Playing the
Short Irons

The seven-, eight-, nine-irons, along with the pitching wedges, are the short irons in the bag of clubs. These clubs are played with much more feel than any others. With short irons a player has a real sense that he is "working" the ball not only onto the green but, perhaps, into the hole!

These clubs are important, too, because with them the middle- and high-handicapper has a chance to recover from a misplayed mid-iron. Hitting a short iron close to the pin can mean an easy par or birdie.

The short irons are also easier clubs to hit because there is not as much body action. And the little body movement involved must be toned down and refined for the shot. Excess motion in your body on such a finesse shot can mean that the ball will go out of control.

Most players move the ball up in their stance, playing it off the left heel or instep. From this position, and with the loft of the blade, the ball will go higher and spin more. This means the shot must be played a lot softer. You want to throw the ball high and have it land softly.

Under normal conditions the ball will not bounce high,

and with a watered green it will only roll ten or fifteen feet. It will not have tremendous backspin. That's only for professionals on television.

But how can you achieve such a backspin with a short iron?

One professional on the Senior Tour who can control this shot is Bobby Nichols. In describing how he hits an eight-iron so it will dance on the green, Nichols points out that of all the irons, these short ones are played close to the body. "I also move the ball back in my stance, playing it more toward the right foot. (Fig. 1.)

(Fig. 1.) *With short irons, play the ball back in the stance.*

"With an eight-iron, I set the ball a little past center. By setting it in this position, I'm able to come into it with a descending blow and catch the ball first and then the turf."

Nichols also sets his hands in the middle of his body. "I kinda use my belly button as a target. Some players, of course, move their hands a little farther forward than I do, but there's a lot of players that use this system and it seems to work best for me." (Fig. 2., 3., 4., 5., 6.)

Nichols points out that what is most important for him on the short irons is that the shaft and the butt end of the club are pointing to his navel. "This enables me to release

FIG. 2.

(Fig. 2.) *Nichols sets the ball past center and with his hands in middle of his body.*

(Fig. 3., 4.) *Nichols hit the ball first, then the turf.*

FIG. 3.

FIG. 4.

FIG. 5.

FIG. 6.

(Fig. 5., 6.) *Stay down and hit through the ball.*

on the ball without creating any angles in the swing," he explains. "If I get my hands too far forward, that creates an angle. But by placing my hands in the middle of the stance, I have the feeling that there's a togetherness between my hands, the club head, and the point where the ball will be struck."

Although the seven- and eight-irons are usually used from 120 to 140 yards, these same clubs are also useful when the ball is closer to the pin, less than 40 yards from the green.

Bob Watson, who has spent the majority of his career as a teaching home professional, points out that many middle-handicap players overlook the use of the seven- and eight-irons when approaching the green from this distance. And he believes that this is a mistake.

Watson believes most golfers fail to learn how to play the game along the ground as well as through the air, and as a result they make the game tougher on themselves.

"If you keep the ball low, you're just going to be more consistent," explains Watson, standing over a ball that is forty yards from the cup. "If you think about it, hitting the ball low is the easiest way to get it in the hole."

Watson's theory is that by playing the approach shot with a straight-face club, the player has many advantages. "The less loft you take with a club, the less swing you need, and the less chance for you to flub the shot. Trying to hit a shot with loft, you might dump it, hit it a few feet, or blade the ball and knock it across the green."

The decision on what club to use from forty or so yards from the green depends mostly on experience. "When a player uses this shot a few times, he'll figure out what club feels the most comfortable."

Watson learned the advantage of such a shot while growing up in West Texas, where the ground was as hard as rock. In those days he used the putter, commonly called the "Texas wedge" because, as he said, "even if I muff a putt it would at least bounce up to the green."

The advantage for Watson, then, is that by using a straighter-faced club, the ball is played along the ground, without a big swing, (Fig. 7.) and even if the club is

(Fig. 7.) *Use a straighter-faced club from a level lie to the pin.*

misplayed on the toe or heel, it has a better chance of ending up close to the hole than the same shot using a wedge.

"The trouble with a lofted club," according to Watson, "a pitching wedge, for example, is that it requires precise timing and precise contact. It is a more demanding shot and the penalty if it doesn't come off is far greater."

A PGA professional on the Senior Tour, Watson points out, has a variety of shots that he might play from the same position. "A good pro might chip it, pitch-and-run the ball, pitch it, or even blast it. He has the repertoire and the judgment to decide what's right for him. But if you're standing here with lots of pressure on you—the chance to win the Westchester Classic, for example—then you'll instinctively go to the straight-faced club, the one easiest to hit."

Watson sets up with the ball in the middle, but his weight, his center of balance, is toward the hole. He does this to assure himself that he won't hit behind the ball. The lowest part of his swing is at the very bottom of the ball and his weight is forward, on his left leg. (Fig. 8.) The shot works for Bob Watson and hundreds of PGA professionals just like him, whether they have come from West Texas or not.

When you are playing out of thick grass, however, or the green isn't open and flat, then, as Gene Littler points out, the wedge comes into play. Most players have just two clubs to consider: the pitching and sand wedge. The differences between these two for Littler is that he is able to make the sand wedge work the ball more. That is, it is more likely to get the ball to bite and not roll.

However, both wedges are played from the middle of his stance. "I want to hit down on the ball," Littler explains, "catching the ball first." (Fig. 9.)

(Fig. 8.) Watson's hands are forward, his weight on his left side.

(Fig. 9.) Littler plays the ball back
in the stance and has his hands
forward.

The blade is open when he addresses the ball, and he does not change the position of his hands, but lets the club catch the ball with its open face (Fig. 10.) so, as he puts it, "I get a high, soft shot." (Fig. 11.)

(Fig. 10.) *The face of the wedge is open.*

(Fig. 11.) *Hit down and through long grass.*

Points to Remember

- *Play the short irons from the middle of the stance.*

    - *Approach the green with less lofted clubs.*

- *Play the wedges with an open club face.*
  - *Take into consideration the grass and contour of the green.*
    - *Develop a variety of shots for around the green.*

BOB GOALBY

BIRTHDATE: March 14, 1929
BIRTHPLACE: Belleville, Illinois
RESIDENCE: Delray Beach, Florida
JOINED PGA TOUR: 1957
PGA TOUR VICTORIES: 11
PGA TOUR CAREER EARNINGS: $645,013
JOINED SENIOR PGA TOUR: 1980
SENIOR TOUR VICTORIES THROUGH 1989: 3
SENIOR TOUR EARNINGS THROUGH 1989: $538,475
CAREER EARNINGS: $1,183,488
BEST YEAR ON PGA TOUR: $58,996 (1970)
BEST YEAR ON SENIOR PGA TOUR: $114,089 (1984)

BOB GOALBY
Golf Analyst

For years Bob Goalby was best known as a golf analyst for NBC, not as a top-flight professional golfer. Goalby, however, is one of the reasons there is a Senior Tour. He was one of the founding members back in 1979 and still serves on the policy board.

The fact that Goalby is still playing is almost as surprising as the fact that he became a professional in the first place. When he was still a teenager, baseball was his first love, and three major league baseball teams wanted to sign him out of high school. Instead Goalby went to play football at the University of Illinois, then sold cars for a living after leaving school. He didn't turn professional until 1957, at the late age of twenty-six.

Playing the tour and winning has never been easy for Bob. He has had a long career with spectacular successes and years of obscurity. He began his golf career, however, with a rush. In 1958 he was named the tour's Rookie-of-the-Year, winning the Greater Greensboro Open, the first of his eleven victories on the regular tour, including the 1968 Masters.

Goalby had never finished better than twenty-fifth at the

Masters, but in 1968 he shot a brilliant finishing round of 66, one of the best in Augusta's history, scoring two birdies and an eagle on three of the finishing holes. The victory, however, was bittersweet. Roberto de Vicenzo, who would have tied him for the tournament, was penalized for signing an incorrect scorecard and Goalby was declared the winner outright. (Fig. 1.)

Goalby came close to winning other major championships. In 1961 he finished second behind Gene Littler at the U.S. Open, and in 1962 he was second to Gary Player at the PGA Championship.

In 1961 he made eight birdies in a row in the final round of the St. Petersburg Open, a Tour record for consecutive birdies that has been equalled but never beaten. Playing on only one Ryder Cup team, Goalby in 1963 at Atlanta won all of his single matches and was also unbeaten in the foursomes.

Always close to winning whenever he was on tour, Goalby was among the top sixty money winners from 1958 to 1963, then again from 1965 to 1973, before retiring from competition to become an NBC golf analyst.

While on tour Goalby was a member of the PGA tournament committee for two years, and it was only natural that he would be involved in 1979 with the creation of the new Senior Tour.

The tour began with just $250,000 and two events, but it has grown beyond anything Bob Goalby expected.

For Goalby, his success in the golf game has been done off the course as well as on it. "I had a little something to do with the success of the Senior Tour, and I'm very proud of that. I'll be on the advisory board through 1990, and that will make eleven years for me. It's really unbelievable when I think how successful we have been with the Senior Tour."

One credit that Goalby can claim is his work with television sponsorship. "In 1980 we had no television broadcast of our few events," he recalls. "No one thought that television wanted us, a bunch of gray-haired guys. We asked the PGA Commissioner if we could try to get the television rights ourselves, and he let us. We sold the first television

(Fig. 1.) *Bob Goalby, proud to have helped make the Senior Tour a reality.*

package to Mazda. And having gotten Mazda, we also signed up Cadillac for something like $18 million over five years. Well, in 1990, we will have twenty-three events broadcast on television, and a large percentage of our $14 million of prize money comes directly from those television rights."

Goalby left NBC after broadcasting for thirteen years because he was tired of traveling and being away from his family. Also, as he added, "I guess I'd rather play golf on the Senior Tour than do anything else. I want to play these last few years. I don't want to give up this time of my life, my few good remaining years, and then say, 'I wish I had played.' I've been in golf, around golf, with golf for too many years not to want to leave the game still swinging a club."

Playing the
Difficult Approach

About six years ago a new approach shot was invented by professional golfers to handle the increasingly thick fringes that they were finding at the aprons of tournament greens. PGA senior pros were discovering that their balls were rolling up against grass one and two inches thick. (Fig. 1.)

This new thick grass was due to the fact that greens and aprons today are being fertilized and receiving more water. When they were to make this delicate shot from the apron, the touring pros were finding a half inch of grass between the ball and club face. The result was a difficult shot. To deal with this new golf course condition—making a short approach shot from a grassy lie—the pros invented a new shot. "They opened the club face of their wedge," Bob Goalby explains. "They stood open, and they hit the ball with the leading edge of the club. This caused the ball to come out of the grass with over-spin and roll up to the hole." (Fig. 2.)

(Fig. 1.) Watered green means thick aprons.

(Fig. 2.) *Strike the ball with the edge of the wedge.*

While the stroke is like a putting stroke, a player does not use any wrist in making the shot. "You're hitting the ball with the narrow point of the leading edge of the club," according to Goalby. "This keeps you from getting a lot of grass between the club face and the ball." It also helps, Bob points out, "that when making the shot, that you not pinch down in the grass, which will kill the club head speed. You're actually just blading the ball with the leading edge of the wedge." (Fig. 3., 4., 5.)

Bob first saw this shot used ten years ago, but it is only

(Fig. 3.–5.) *Catch the ball, not the grass.*

within the last five years that it has become prevalent on tour.

"It scares you at first," admits Goalby, "and it takes a little practice to hit it correctly, but once a player has worked on the shot and finds himself in a situation where the grass is thick and you'll never be able to get the club face on the ball, this shot is the perfect choice."

The way to play the shot, remember, is to just stand open, open the blade of the wedge a little, and, using a putting stroke, make contact with the ball.

The modern golf courses also have lush fairways that present more problems for approach shots to the green. Bob Goalby moved ten yards away from the green to demonstrate how to play an approach from deep, thick grass, again with the wedge.

Bob admits that this approach shot with a wedge is one of the most difficult in golf, because a player can't chip the ball from such long grass. "What you're trying to do," explains Goalby, "is to swing a little too hard, so as to get through the thick grass, and to make you follow through on the shot." (Fig. 6.)

(Fig. 6.) *Hit down and through the ball.*

Think of this approach shot from deep grass as you would think of hitting a sand shot. First open the stance, then hit behind the ball about two inches, and follow through by letting the club slide under the ball. Even though you are swinging too hard, the grass will kill the club head speed. But the follow-through will pick the ball up and out, almost, according to Goalby, "like an ice cream scoop."

One way to remember how much to open your stance is to match it with the club face. If you open the blade thirty degrees, then you open your hip thirty degrees. If you open it forty-five, you open your hips forty-five. As Goalby points out, this will allow you to go through and get your left hip out of the way as well as keeping the blade square. "If you square your body to the target and then swing, the club face will be closed at impact and you won't get the needed action on the club face. However, if you swing with an open stance, your left hip will be out of the way and the club face will be square to the target." (Fig. 7.)

According to Goalby, the problem average players have is that they are afraid to open the blade of the club, or they do it while being square to the line of flight.

What is also important with this shot is the condition of the grass. If it is wet and long, the club will likely become trapped in it. So check the condition of the grass before making the shot. Brown grass means that the shot will not require as much effort; the greener and thicker the grass, the more effort it will take to pop out the ball. "It is all a matter of experience, of playing on different types of grass, and of learning what works for you," Goalby sums up. "A player needs to learn the conditions of the grass, much as the way he has to learn, by testing the sand with his feet, how wet the sand is."

Once the player is set on the type of grass that is being

(Fig. 7.) *Open stance, left hip out of the way.*

played from, then check out the grain and slope of the green.

If playing from a downhill lie, Goalby sets the ball farther back in his stance and has his shoulders match the contour of the hill. "You don't want to put all of your weight on the right side to try to help the ball in the air. Rather, you have to join the contour of the hill while opening your stance." (Fig. 8.)

The reason is that on a downhill lie, the ball will have a tendency to slice coming out of the grass. So the answer is to open your stance and aim a little more to the left. "As you swing," Goalby points out, "keep your weight on your left side. Don't try to sway it back to the right because that will make the lower point of your arc catch the hill behind the ball."

When Bob swings, he makes sure to hit the ball first and

(Fig. 8.) *Join the contour of the hill.*

then swing down the contour of the hill. "Stay with the hill," he reminds us, "don't try to help lift or scoop the ball off. The worst thing a player can do is drop his right shoulder. If you need a little more loft, then take a little more club because it's going to come off this shot lower than normal. If it is a seven-iron shot, you can take the eight-iron, and the ball will come off the lie with a seven-iron loft, and it will go farther because it's coming off with a lower trajectory."

Given the same sort of shot with an uphill lie, Goalby squares himself up to the ball and aims to the right of the target. (Fig. 9.) He also chokes up on the grip. "The first rule is choking up on the club so as not to hit the shot fat." On a shot like this—with the feet below the ball—the

(Fig. 9.) *Keep square to the target.*

weight of the body naturally goes to the heels, and when the swing is made, players have a tendency to fall backward, which causes the ball to be hooked."

The player should set up anticipating this by aiming to the right and playing the ball farther back in the stance. The points to remember are choking up on the grip, aiming to the right, and not swinging too hard. Bob Goalby points out that if the shot calls for a seven-iron, then take an extra club, a six-iron, and swing softer, which will allow you to maintain better balance. Goalby also reminds us that "if you swing real hard, you'll fall backward more and hook the shot."

An additional problem with such an uphill lie is that the average player never seems to get to the hole with his ball. The tendency with such an approach shot, using either a pitching or sand wedge, is that a player will swing with the contour of the hill. This naturally adds four-to-five degrees of loft to the club. The result is that the ball comes up short. Goalby suggests that players go to an eight- or nine-iron for this shot and play the ball in the middle of the stance.

"All a player has to remember," he points out, "is that on uphill lies, take less loft clubs, and on downhill, add loft to the club selection. And in both positions, swing the club like a wedge, making sure to hit the ball first."

Points to Remember

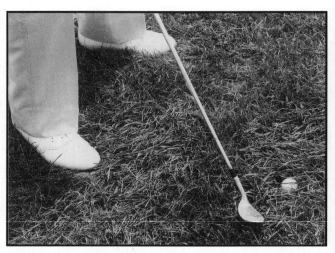

APPROACH FROM THICK, GRASSY APRON	APPROACH SHOT FROM DEEP GRASS
• *Use a wedge.* • *Stance open.* • *Use a putting stroke.*	• *Use a wedge.* • *Stance open.* • *Open the blade.* • *Hit the ball as if coming out of sand.* • *Follow through.*

PLAYING FROM
A DOWNHILL LIE

- *Weight on left side.*
- *Open stance.*
- *Follow contour of the hill.*
- *Aim left.*
- *Swing down the contour.*

PLAYING FROM
AN UPHILL LIE

- *Choke up.*
- *Aim right.*
- *Play the ball back in the stance.*
- *Swing soft.*
- *Use more club.*

Playing Out
of Trouble

One of the most difficult shots for all players is when he is stymied behind a tree, either off the fairway or close to the green. Good players are good scramblers. They are able to manufacture a shot that gets them out of tight positions.

Bob Goalby is one player on the Senior Tour who knows how to save a shot, as well as strokes, regardless of where his ball ends up on the golf course.

To show how to play one such spot, Bob moved his ball a hundred and fifty yards back down the fairway, where his shot would be partially blocked by a low branch.

"Now, here's where I can't get the ball elevated for the distance I need to reach the green," Bob explains. "I'm forced to hit a little punch, a trick shot under his limb. (Fig. 1.) The first thing I have to do is select the right club. Then I have to decide how hard I have to hit it to get to the green."

(Fig. 1.) *Shot needs to be kept low and long.*

Having made these decisions, Bob sets up for the shot. He opens his stance and plays the ball from back in his stance, off his right foot. "I want to catch the ball going down and through, and I want to ride my hands through the shot. I don't want to release my hands at impact because that will let the ball go up in the air. I actually hood the club somewhat so the ball comes out with a lower trajectory." (Fig. 2., 3.)

(Fig. 2., 3.) Don't release the hands and hood the club face.

Goalby also is aware that the ball will come out "hot" and run on the level-cut fairway, so he takes into consideration how far the ball might roll. "I play short of the green and realize the ball will run for perhaps another twenty yards. What I need to know, of course, is how hard the ground is around the green. That's why you'll see professionals walking up to the green before they hit a low-trajectory shot. They know the ball will run, and they need to calculate how many yards they'll pick up with that roll. And that will affect how hard they'll hit the ball."

When playing a shot from under a limb, you need to remember a few basic points:

Play the ball back in your open stance. Open your stance because you're going to take a three-quarters backswing and a three-quarter follow-through. With this little punch stroke, you need to get your left hip out of the way. So at the address, open the stance, play the ball toward the middle of the stance, and hood the club slightly to take more of the loft off the club and cause a lower trajectory.

Lastly, hit the ball with your hands riding forward. This will restrict your follow-through and allow you to follow the contour of the ground. (Fig. 4., 5., 6.)

A similar shot is required when the ball is under a tree but closer to the green. Here the problem is that you cannot hit a low, "hot" shot, or use the yardage of the fairway to your advantage.

Bob Watson plays this shot near the green with a long iron, which won't have much loft, but will give him the slight roll he needs to get the ball close to the pin.

"The length of my swing can best be envisioned by thinking of a pendulum of a clock," Watson explains. "For a short swing, I might go back to eight o'clock and then hit through to four o'clock. I have learned how far the ball

FIG. 4.

FIG. 5.

FIG. 6.

(Fig. 4., 5., 6.) *Hit the ball with your hands, following the contour.*

will run after I hit it from years of practice. I have also learned what club feels most natural to me. Once a player gains this touch, knows what club is right, then the shot is actually very simple." (Fig. 7.)

One problem most players have is that they don't realize that when they hit down on a ball—in an attempt to keep it low—the ball will bounce up on them. That is why a low-lofted club and a smooth swing is necessary. "If you're going to make a mistake," Watson advises, "make it with a less lofted club."

Also, according to Watson, "You have to remember that a ball tends to get higher in the air than you might think. Try to get into the habit of playing with a one less club than you think is necessary for a shot like this one."

Again the ball is played with very little body motion from an open stance. The ball position in the stance is off the left heel. The hands and arms work with one action and the simple pendulum stroke will pick the ball off the rough ground, carry it over the long grass, and let it land on the apron or just on the green, so the ball will have the chance to roll toward the pin.

(Fig. 7.) Watson uses a short swing and a club without loft in such a position, letting the ball roll toward the cup.

Points to Remember

- Right club for distance.

- Open stance.

- Play the ball in the middle of the stance.

- Short backswing and follow-through.

- Hood the club face.

- Place the hand forward.

JIM FERREE

BIRTHDATE: June 10, 1931

BIRTHPLACE: Pine Bluff,
   North Carolina

RESIDENCE: Hilton Head, South Carolina

JOINED PGA TOUR: 1956

PGA TOUR VICTORIES: 1

PGA TOUR CAREER EARNINGS: $107,719

JOINED SENIOR PGA TOUR: 1981

SENIOR TOUR VICTORIES THROUGH 1989: 1

SENIOR TOUR EARNINGS THROUGH 1989: $768,161

CAREER EARNINGS: $875,880

BEST YEAR ON PGA TOUR: $16,638 (1959)

BEST YEAR ON SENIOR PGA TOUR: $184,667 (1987)

JIM FERREE
The Dapper Dresser

Son of the legendary home professional, Purvis Ferree, Jim turned professional in 1956 and played eleven years on the regular PGA Tour. Considered one of the greatest players to come out of the University of North Carolina, Ferree won only once on the regular PGA Tour, when he carved an 11-under-par 61 in the second round of the 1958 Vancouver Centennial on his way to winning by one stroke over Billy Casper. Ferree also won three times on the old Caribbean Tour in the early 1960s, before quitting the tour in 1966 to become a home professional at Hilton Head Island in South Carolina.

Ferree's problems on the PGA Tour were his putter and a lifetime of what he called the "yip." All of this changed. however, when he came on the Senior Tour and discovered the new long putter.

"I was playing with Charlie Owens, who was the first person who started using the long putter on tour. Charlie was just a terrible putter and I figured if he could putt with it, so could I.

(Fig. 1.) Jim Ferree has been saved on the Senior Tour by using the long putter.

"Charlie was nice enough to give me a spare putter, like the ones he uses—a Slim Jim—and I took it back to Hilton Head and didn't play for two weeks. I just practiced a couple hours every day and then I went up to the TPC Championship, which was held at Canterbury that year, and they have very difficult greens. I thought, well, if the long putter works here, it will work anywhere."

Ferree went out and played in the pro-am before the tournament started and shot 68. "Now, that round came after a long period of time where the best I could shoot would be either a 73 or 74."

Ferree finished fourteenth in the TPC and the next week at the U.S. Seniors Open he finished sixth. The following week at Greenbriar, he tied Don January for first and then lost in the playoff. One week later in Grand Rapids, Michigan, he tied Chi Chi Rodriguez and Gene Littler for first. Then he birdied the first hole of the playoff. In four weeks of using his new long putter, he had two firsts, a sixth, and a fourteenth. The new putter has given Jim Ferree a second chance at playing competitive golf.

Ferree doesn't think that the long putter has meant a psychological change for him, but believes that it's the "nature of the beast" that has helped him.

"The long putter is much heavier than a short one, and that makes a big difference. Also, I stand up more erect, which is certainly a more relaxed position than being cramped over, leaning down over a short one, and trying to hold dead still."

Getting adjusted to the long putter took Jim Ferree only twelve hours of practice. What Ferree had to do was get comfortable with the new putter and his new stance. Once he was comfortable standing over the ball, then it was just a matter of learning to putt long putts. For Ferree it has been "smooth sailing" ever since. (Fig. 1.)

Jim doesn't know if the long putter will become the predominant putter on tour or at the local country club. "It depends whether a player needs the putter to improve his game, and if he can swallow his pride to use it." But for Ferree, "It would be fine if nobody else used it because everyone who starts putting with it does so well. I'd love for nobody else to putt with the thing."

Ferree still has bad rounds with the putter, but he's not faulting it. It has been winning money on the Senior Tour, and better still, it kept away the "yips."

Playing Out of Sand

Playing from the sand trap is one of the easier shots on the golf course, but most players don't believe it. The fact is, when you play from the sand, you don't even want to hit the ball! A sand shot requires less golf skill but more practice.

What is the key, however, and the reason that most players don't get their ball out of the trap, over the lip, and onto the green is that they don't use the correct stance. They don't open themselves to the shot. And you can never be too open for a bunker shot.

As Jim Ferree explains it, "I play the shot from an open stance, and I aim slightly left of the target. (Fig. 1.) This permits the club face to be open when it slides underneath the ball."

The reason the bunker shot is easy is because the shot allows for error. If you catch the ball heavy, it will run a little more; if you catch it thin, it will bite. Ferree sums up, saying, "What you are doing with this bunker shot is simply displacing sand. The ball doesn't come in contact with the club face. It simply rides out of the sand, on sand."

(Fig. 1.) Play the shot from an open stance.

To get the club face in the right position, Ferree first lays the wedge open and then places his hands on the club. "I do this," he explains, "because when I swing, I want the club face to stay in the same position." If he started with the club face square and then tilted his hands to the right for an open hand position, the tendency of his hands would be to come back to square during his swing and at impact.

Another adjustment that Jim makes is in his stance. "On a normal shot, you try to get your right shoulder lower than your left, but when playing from the bunker, keep your shoulders level with a lot more weight on your left side." (Fig. 2.)

(Fig. 2.) *Shoulders level, weight on the left side.*

Addressing the ball, Ferree pulls his left foot off the line at least ten inches to establish his open position. Because the shot is played with the shortest club in the bag, he stands close to the ball, and uses a swing with a much more upright plane. His arms and hands are not clamped

FIG. 3.

FIG. 4.

tight against his side. In fact, the trademark of this shot is a very loose swing, as well as a loose grip on the club. The shot is hit easy. He takes the club back in a slow, smooth stroke, as if he were pitching a softball. Then he throws his right hand through the ball just as if he had a softball and

FIG. 5.

FIG. 6.

were pitching it toward the plate. There is no need to try and hit the ball hard because a ball coming out of soft sand might run thirty feet on a flat, hard green. (Fig. 3., 4., 5., 6., 7., 8.)

FIG. 7.

FIG. 8.

(Fig. 3.–8.) *Hit the shot as if you were throwing a softball.*

"If you really want to become a good sand player," Ferree advises, "you need to get into the sand trap and draw a line an inch behind the ball and practice hitting from that line. If you don't draw a line in the sand, you won't know whether you are hitting three inches behind the ball or two inches.

"I've always believed in using such visual aids when I'm practicing. Quite often you might think that you're not hitting hard enough, but what you'll discover is that you are actually hitting four inches behind the ball. You can't possibly move that much sand and still hit the ball."

Playing from the sand also means knowing the condition of the sand. When sand is wet, for example, the club head will bounce. A player needs to catch the ball thin to make this shot. In such conditions it is often better to use the pitching wedge. The pitching wedge is not as heavy as the sand wedge and is less likely to bounce off wet sand.

If the ball is buried, or plugged, then the bunker shot has to be hit entirely differently. First get square to the ball and hood the wedge face. When the blade hits the sand, the club face will open. Also break the wrist slightly on the backswing and take the club more to the outside. On this shot you should release your hands a little more quickly on the downswing and bring the club head down behind the ball about two inches. This abrupt motion of the club will make the ball pop out of the sand. The ball, coming from a plugged lie, will also run more on the green.

Regardless of the condition of the sand or the lie, don't quit on the sand shot. While the sand wedge is hit with a soft swing, you can't get lazy or stop your follow-through. Get in the habit of practicing sweeping the club back and forth rhythmically, and stopping on the backswing or at impact. Once you have the correct feel, you won't be intimidated when you get set to hit the ball.

Ferree sums up playing the bunker shot this way: "After I determine the type of sand, I stand with my feet slightly open to the target. I'm aiming to the left as well as having my feet and body position left. (Fig. 9.) I set the face of the club open when I grip the club so it's pointing toward the target. I stand with about eighty percent of my weight on my left foot at the address, and try to keep my shoulders level. Level shoulders will encourage the club to come up much more abruptly than it does from a normal stance. I want the club to come up in the air because I don't want a big, wide, long arc of a swing. You can't hit the ball short enough with a wide arc. I grip down on the club, and that will shorten my swing even more. I also play the ball toward the center of my stance; otherwise the club is trying to travel upward as I'm trying to hit under the ball." (Fig. 10.)

If you are serious about playing well, you need to carry in the bag both the sand and pitching wedges. The sand wedge has a large flange, more head weight, and greater loft than any other club. It's designed to do one job only: to get you out of the sand. If you play with only a pitching wedge you are giving yourself an additional handicap.

The pitching wedge is very useful and necessary, but it isn't the right club for getting out of the sand.

(Fig. 9.) *At the address, be to the left of the target.*

(Fig. 10.) *Ball is in the middle of the stance.*

Points to Remember

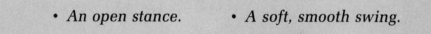

• *An open stance.*   • *A soft, smooth swing.*

- *Hit one to two inches behind the ball.*

- *Don't quit on the shot.*

Playing with
the Long Putter

The most revolutionary "new" golf club to appear in the last few years is the long putter. It is not a gimmick club, and, I believe, it will change the way the next generation of players putt. (Fig. 1.)

When Orville Moody used the long putter to win the 1989 U.S. Senior Open, the United States Golf Association, which sets the standards for golf equipment, took notice and considered a proposal to limit the length of a putter, feeling that the long putter was not conforming to the traditional style of club.

Yet when they reviewed the use of the long putter, they realized that this type of putter was actually first used over thirty years ago by the golfing great Paul Runyan, a former PGA champion famous for his chipping and putting.

In September 1989, USGA decided that if long putters enabled more people to play without jeopardizing the integrity of the game, it should be continued. "Putting is a very individual art form," remarked David Fay, USGA Executive Director. "To inhibit a golfer's individual style would take some of the fun out of the game, and that's not why we make rules."

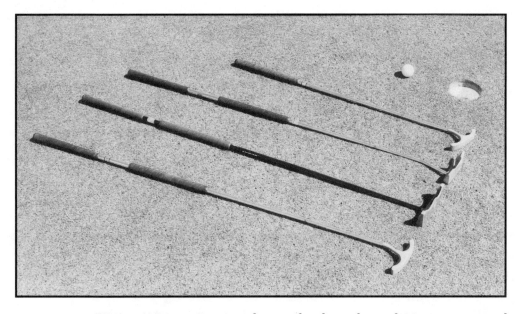

(Fig. 1.) *Long Putters have the length and size compared to traditional putter.*

The USGA had come down on the right side of the issue, for the long putter is making a lot of golfers better players. The president and the vice-president of the United States now both use a type of the long putter. Last summer at Kennebunkport, Maine, Ken Raynor, the golf professional at Cape Arundel Golf Club, where President Bush plays, watched the president sink a putt with a long putter on the first hole.

"It was a 20-footer and he put it right into the jar. A big smile came over his face, and for the rest of the day he sank putts from all over the place."

The putter was made by a small Orlando-based golf equipment company, Kiti & Taylor Enterprises, who had sent the putter as a gift to the president after Kitione Maile, a partner in Kiti & Taylor Enterprises, had heard the president was suffering from the "yips."

The president used their 52-inch Pole-Kat putter over the Fourth of July weekend. Raynor reported back that the president shot 81 that day, his best score in years. "All of a sudden," Raynor told Kitione Maile, "the president was enjoying golf again."

And this is true all over the country. Golfers are smiling with their successes with the long putter.

John Rouzee Green, of York, South Carolina, owner of the Old Master Company, has been designing and manufacturing putters since the early 1960s, and was, with the Positive Putter Company of Indianapolis, Indiana, one of the first companies to begin to manufacture the long putter.

It is John Green who developed one method of using the long putter, which, at first, appears daunting.

"What a player has to remember," according to Green, "is that the reason to use the long putter is because it takes less coordination and fewer muscles. Therefore, there is less chance for errors."

The simple stroke used in the long putter—a pendulum—and the fact that the length allows a player to stand more upright, giving him more peripheral vision and less need to rotate the head for lining-up purposes, account for golfers putting better.

A player should select a putter that is about two-thirds his height. What is important is that the shaft of the club be short enough so that the player can get his head and shoulders over the top of the putter and ball.

The majority of long putters have split grips and require a split-hand position on the club. The left hand, for right-handed players, is at the top, using a reverse grip. (Fig. 2.) The left thumb might also be placed on top of the shaft.

The top of the putter is at chest height and positioned snugly against the chest, (Fig. 3.) playing the ball slightly

(Fig. 2.) *The left hand is at the top of the shaft.*

(Fig. 3.) Putter is pressed snugly against the chest.

ahead in the stance. One variation of this is, according to John Green, "to pin the heel of your left hand in the center of your left breast with the wrist rotated so the back of the hand is perpendicular to the intended line of the putt. This allows the top of the shaft to be some three-quarters of an inch away from the body. It is helpful to players with fuller figures who need the free right-arm movement."

Played this way, the ball should be placed closer to the left toe. And in both positions, the ball should be hit on the upswing, which will make the ball roll correctly.

The right hand should extend down the shaft of the club to its most comfortable position, but with some bend to the elbow. The fingers of the right hand can be set in the most comfortable position for the individual. The finger can be down the shaft, (Fig. 4.) set between the first two fingers (Fig. 5) or simply held like a normal grip of the right hand (Fig. 6.), but in all situations the grip should pass through the U in the hand created by the heel of the palm and the base of the thumb. (Fig. 7.) The club is held lightly with the right hand so the stroke will be even and true.

Generally, the ball should be set close to the toes when standing over the putt. (Fig. 8.) This will help establish a true pendulum stroke. Once in position, keep the upper body steady so as to eliminate any movement, which can cause the player to pull or push the putt.

Jim Ferree was one of the first players on the Senior Tour to use the long putter, following the example set by Charlie Owens, who had won two tournaments on the Senior tour with the new club.

"Charlie was an awful putter," recalls Ferree, "and I thought that if it could help Charlie, it might help me."

Ferree had quit the professional tour in 1966 because of his inability to putt. "I had the yips," recalls Ferree, "and

(Fig. 4.) *The finger is down the shaft.* (Fig. 5.) *Or set between two fingers.*

they stayed with me for a long time. Even when I started to play on the Senior Tour in 1986, the yips came back and I couldn't make a putt.''

Ferree still has bad rounds with the putter, but it is not the club that is at fault, rather the green or his failure to putt well. He does know that he sees the line better by standing tall.

Ferree's putter is fifty inches long. Charlie Owens putts

(Fig. 6.) *Or held with a normal grip by the right hand.*

(Fig. 7.) *But in all cases, the club should pass through the U created by the heel of the palm and the base of the thumb.*

with one that is fifty-two inches long; Charlie Cootie's is fifty-one inches, while Don Bies is forty-seven inches. "It just depends on your height and what you feel comfortable with. Every now and then I change to a putter that is forty-eight inches, but I find that I continually come back to my fifty incher."

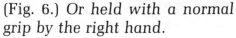

Ferree has found that by using the long putter, he is able to get a better read of the green, seeing the line better once he has addressed the ball. Also by "standing" at the putt, he finds that he is steadier over the ball. (Fig. 9.) "One thing about the long putter," according to Ferree, "is that

(Fig. 8.) *The ball is positioned close to the feet.*

(Fig. 9.) *By standing at the ball, the player is steadier over the putt.*

anyone with ball trouble who practices a lot this way won't get tired. For a person with back problems, putting can be very strenuous. The long putter helps solve that problem."

Bob Watson is another golf professional who has switched to the long putter when his nerves became unreliable, particularly on short putts. "I tried everything," Watson recalls. "I putted left-handed, cross-handed. I even tried to putt with my eyes closed, but I still had the 'yips,' so I experimented with this long putter."

Watson has switched to the long putter for several reasons. "As a tall person with a bad back, the long putter lets me stand taller and practice longer. And for the first time I felt that my arms were truly extended on the club. Also, under pressure, the long putter let me rotate my shoulders without any arm or hand motion. The only place that I don't use it is on long putts with a slow green. I just can't get the solid contact with the long stroke needed for that putt. But otherwise the long putter has been a godsend."

Watson holds the top of the putter with his left hand close to his body and taut against the left side of his chest, then reaches down as far as he can with his right hand so that his arm is extended and there is no independent motion of his right wrist.

"I place the top of the club against the left side of my chest," Watson points out, "because if it is set in the center of the chest, there is a tendency to rotate the shoulders. The club face then will close and pull to the left of center." (Fig. 10.)

By extending the right arm as far as he can, Watson also freezes the right side, making it firm. There is then one solid, swinging motion of the club. (Fig. 11.)

In general, putting with the long putter is no different than putting with any other style of putter.

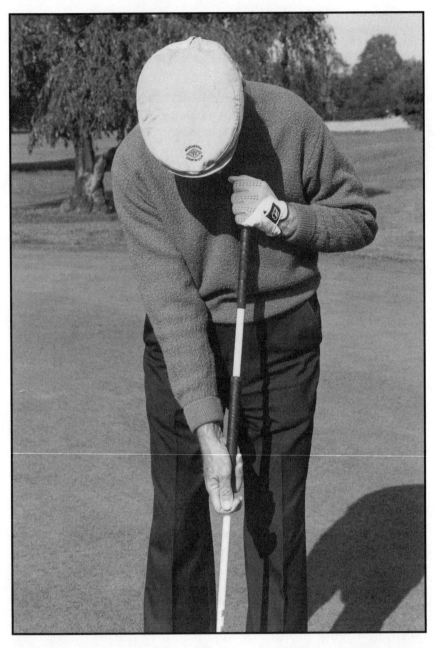

(Fig. 10.) Place the top of the club against the left side of the chest.

Points to Remember

- *Practice putting before playing.*

- *Once over the ball, keep your head steady.*

- *Take a short backstroke and accelerate through the ball.*

- *Strike the ball on the upswing.*

RECOMMENDED LENGTHS FOR THE LONG PUTTER

Putter Length	Player Height
36″	4′6″
38″	4′9″
40″	5′
42″	5′3″
44″	5′6″
46″	5′9″
48″	6′
50″	6′3″
52″	6′6″

GENE LITTLER

BIRTHDATE: July 21, 1930
BIRTHPLACE: San Diego,
    California
RESIDENCE: Rancho Santa Fe, California
JOINED PGA TOUR: 1954
PGA TOUR VICTORIES: 29
PGA TOUR CAREER EARNINGS: $1,578,625
JOINED SENIOR PGA TOUR: 1981
SENIOR TOUR VICTORIES THROUGH 1989: 8
SENIOR TOUR EARNINGS THROUGH 1989: $1,473,877
CAREER EARNINGS: $2,801,786
BEST YEAR ON PGA TOUR: $182,883 (1975)
BEST YEAR ON SENIOR PGA TOUR: $293,195 (1987)

GENE LITTLER
The Machine

Gene Littler is another great player who came out of San Diego in the mid-Fifties to make a name for himself on the PGA tour. Called "Gene the Machine" for his wonderfully smooth swing and his ability to keep the ball always on the fairway, Littler was, early in his career, picked as the likely successor to Ben Hogan.

His golf swing—then and now—is an effortless arc of pure, simple rhythm, a swing that makes golf seem to be the easiest sport in the world to play. Watching him, most people think that they, too, could be a professional golfer. Gene Littler makes golf look like a simple game.

Gene won his first major tournament, the San Diego Open, in 1954, when he was still an amateur. He won his last regular PGA event in 1977, having won twenty-nine times on tour. Only Sam Snead and Jack Nicklaus have more victories over a longer span of time. Littler was also a member of the U.S. Ryder Cup team for ten straight years, from 1961 to 1971.

In 1981 he joined the Senior Tour and immediately won

(Fig. 1.) Littler still has his great smooth swing and his
perfect touch on the green.

the World Seniors Invitational. In the nine years that he has played on the Senior Tour, he has won over $1,500,000.

Many followers of the game feel that Littler would have won more championships, on both tours, if golf had been his primary interest. Littler always, however, wanted to return home to La Jolla, California, to his wife and family, and to his hobby of collecting antique cars, especially Rolls-Royces, which he works on himself and keeps in running order.

Littler continues to play the Senior Tour because, as he says, "It keeps me doing something." And adds, "We're all competitive by nature and the competition is great. At our age it's really nice to be doing something in a physical way."

Littler plans to play on the Senior Tour as long as he is fit. "If it comes to a point when I'm not competitive on this tour, I'll probably find something else to do."

Reaching the point where he is not competitive may take a few more years. Littler still has the basic swing that he first brought to the tour in 1955. Even surgery for cancer of the lymph glands in 1972 did not change it. "I lost some muscles on my left side," Littler recalls, "but it didn't change my swing. All my life, I have basically tried to hit the ball the same way." (Fig. 1.)

Playing with
the Traditional Putter

While the long putter is sweeping the ranks of the Senior Tour, as well as most of the pro shops in the country, there are those great golfers who will not change their putting stroke or their putter. Always the traditionalist, Littler has never changed his putting style, nor succumbed to the rush for a long putter.

"I guess," he says, "I've never had the 'yips.' "

Long known as a brilliant putter, Gene explains how he putts and how anyone can improve their putting stroke without going to the long putter.

"The most important aspect of good putting is keeping everything square. You square your feet. You square your body. And you square your putter. My weight also is basically square, though I might have a little more weight on my left side than I do on my right when I stand over the ball. (Fig. 1.)

"Next, I make a straight stroke back and a straight stroke forward, doing it with very little hand action." (Fig. 2.)

Littler is convinced that golfers get into trouble when they add some wrist action to their putts, and that as they get older, this wrist action develops into the "yips."

(Fig. 1.) *Set yourself square to the ball.*   (Fig. 2.) *Straight stroke, no wrists.*

"I like to have no wrist action at all," says Littler. "I want my arms and wrists to remain as one unit—together—so there's no twitching or slapping at the ball. The putt is a stroke, not a tap or a hit."

Standing over the putt, Littler concentrates on the number on the ball. "I set the number up on the ball when I replace it on the green after cleaning, so I'm hitting the number, that's all, and I concentrate on that spot." (Fig. 3.)

For Littler, how hard to hit the putt is based almost solely on the "feel" he has gained from years of practice. He doesn't take the putter back a certain number of inches for a twelve-foot putt or farther back if the putt is longer. He believes that long putts are more difficult for players who have wrist action in their putts. "That's one reason I stroke the ball the way I do. Over the years I've found that I don't three-putt very often, so I must be doing something right."

Regardless of one's putting stroke, it's important that you are comfortable over the ball, which usually means that the weight is equal on both feet, and between the toe and the heel of each foot.

All professionals, though they have varied styles, use a short, smooth stroke—a putting stroke with perfect cadence. They take the club back low to the ground and accelerate through the ball on the stroke-through. The accelerated stroke creates topspin when the ball is hit—and achieving over-spin gives the ball greater accuracy. The ball holds the line better. This is especially important in the last few inches of a putt when the ball is nearing the hole and is usually losing speed.

It is often said that golfers lose their touch on the green as they get older and when their legs weaken, just like the careers of boxers and tennis players are diminished when they can no longer run.

(Fig. 3.) Concentrate on the back of the ball.

Littler disagrees. "I think you need strong legs to hit a ball on the fairway and off the tee, but I don't think your legs give you a lot of power in the sense of strictly power. They give you power because you set yourself up in the right hitting position to get that power. They themselves don't offer you any power. You can look at somebody like Charlie Owens, who has no legs, and he still hits the ball farther than most of us. The only power you derive from your legs is because your legs set you up to get power from other sources."

Watching Senior Tour players, one is struck how often you see them on the putting green, often practicing before as well as after a round of golf.

Some pros will work on one type of putt—a three-footer, for instance—until by repetition they build up confidence at that length, and on the type of greens they are playing.

The particular type of practice is not as important as establishing a routine of spending at least ten minutes working on putting every time before playing. Ten solid minutes of putting, concentrating on each putt, is much more worthwhile than an hour spent idly putting and talking.

As with all other golf shots, confidence is key. Nothing helps your putting game more than having confidence that you'll make every single putt. Having such confidence in your putting keeps you relaxed and helps establish that smooth stroke.

Also, think positively when you are on the green. Forget what you did the last hole, or how you might have missed a sure putt. Believe in yourself. Believe in your putter. The odds are that you'll make that next putt!

Points to Remember

- *Square to the ball.*

- *No wrist action.*

- *Straight, smooth stroke.*

- *Putt over a spot.*

- *Accelerate through the putt.*

- *Stay confident.*

Playing by Plumb Putting

One of the most accurate ways of "seeing" a putt is to align the slope by plumbing the line. This method is used by many professional players as well as by most fine amateur golfers. It is easy to learn and it will help your game.

Begin by determining your dominant eye, because all plumbing is done with the dominant eye, not from the center of the face. If you don't know your dominant eye, pick out a distant object, hold out your hand, form a circle with your thumb and forefinger, and focus on this object with both eyes. Now close your left eye. If the object is still in the center of the circle, your dominant eye is your right one. If it isn't, your dominate eye is your left one. (Fig. 1.)

In lining up a putt, first move six to eight feet behind the ball and survey the slope of the green. You will be plumbing the putt from about two feet behind the ball, and you want to make sure that the slope is approximately the same throughout the distance to the hole.

Now stand erect two feet behind the ball and face the

(Fig. 1.) *Sight with the dominant eye.*

cup. Make sure you spread your feet and lock your knees
so as to keep your balance. If your body is off-center, so
will your reading of the putt.

It is important to remember that the amount of break
you plumb will vary, depending upon how far you stand
behind the ball. If you are one foot behind, you will plumb
approximately sixty percent more break than at two feet. It
is important to stay at the same distance each time. The
amount of break plumbed while standing two feet behind
the ball on a medium-speed green is based on a firm-type

putt, one in which the ball would stop one foot past the cup.

Standing two feet behind the ball, align the ball and cup with your dominant eye, moving your entire body to the left or right, if needed.

Now hold the putter with your thumb and forefinger as lightly as possible and let the head swing free. When it stops swinging, the plumb is true. (Fig. 2.)

(Fig. 2.) *Hold the putter with your thumb and forefinger.*

Naturally, if you are standing in a spot where there is more slope, this will affect your reading. Generally, if there is more slope where you are standing, you'll want to play less break than you plumb. If there is less slope at your position than at the cup, you will want to play more break than you plumb.

When you have made sure that the lower portion of the shaft of the vertical putter is over the middle of the ball, look at the cup. If you are on a perfectly flat green, the center of the shaft and the center of the cup will be perfectly matched, one over the other. Any amount to the left or the right of the center of the cup is the amount the ball will break.

Having done this, mark the spot of the break in your mind and then stroke the ball toward this spot and not the cup.

With longer and double-breaking putts, it is difficult to get an accurate read of the green, but you'll have a better idea of how much the ball with break in either direction.

Generally, the shorter the putt, the more accurate the plumb. The longer the putt, the less likely you will read all the slopes of the green. (Fig. 3.)

Also, you may have to adjust how far you stand behind the ball if you find your putts are breaking more or less than you plumb.

To help you read the greens, there are a few other important points to remember. See which way the grain is running. If when you look down at the green, you see the grass is dark, you are putting against the grain; therefore, the ball has to be hit harder. If the grass appears glassy and slick, then you are putting with the grain and the ball will run.

A ball hit on a fast green will tend not to take the break, passing over any subtle slopes. Gauging your breaks, then, depends on the grain and on how fast you are stroking the ball.

Before you putt, learn from your playing partners. Pay attention to what is happening on the green. Watch others make their longer putts; this is called "going to school."

Watch the way the ball reacts on the green, especially the speed of the putt. If someone is putting from the same general line as your ball, watch the break, especially within the last few inches of the cup. Often a putt will fall off in the last inches when it is losing speed. Striking the putt with over-spin will help to prevent this.

Points to Remember

- *Use your dominant eye to align the ball and cup.*

- *Make sure your putter is hanging in an exactly vertical (plumb) position.*

- *Stand approximately two feet behind the ball.*

- *Stand erect.*

- *Check the slope and mark the spot.*

- *"Go to school" while your playing partners putt.*

Playing Fit

In 1986 the Centinela Hospital Medical Center of Inglewood, California, began to sponsor a mobile training center for the Senior Tour. These mobile units, also used on the regular PGA Tour and the LPGA Tour, are one of the most popular innovations to appear in recent years.

These impressive training centers contain state-of-the-art exercise equipment in five hundred square feet of carpeted floor space for workout and therapy. The mobile fitness centers are staffed with physical therapists and athletic trainers, and travel with the tour across the country, providing both rehabilitative and preventative care to the professionals at the tournament sites.

The Centinela fitness centers are directed by Dr. Frank Jobe, an orthopedic surgeon and one of the best-known sports physicians, who in 1986 published a book, *30 Exercises for Better Golf*, based on research and tests conducted at the Centinela Hospital Medical Center.

The Centinela Hospital Biomechanics Lab evaluated eight male golfers whose average age was thirty-six. Four of them were touring professionals, two were golf instructors, and two were long-distance drivers.

All of the players were tested the same way, using a modern procedure called electromyography. This procedure is based on the fact that whenever a muscle contracts, it gives off microvolts of electricity. Researchers can record this as a sign of activity.

Each player swung the club four times to test a particular set of muscles on the right side. The testing equipment was then transferred to the left side, and the entire testing procedure was repeated. The first study dealt with shoulder muscle activity—the deltoid, rotator cuff, and several other shoulder-girdle muscles. The next study was the eight muscles in the hip.

The results of this study are interesting to anyone who plays golf and wants to understand the swing. The six conclusions that Dr. Frank W. Jobe and his staff reached, as outlined in his book, are:

1. A good golf swing has bilateral activity.

By studying both the right and left sides during the swing, we found that the golf swing is a balanced activity; the timing and the sequencing alternative, but the net muscular output shows as much activity on the left side as on the right. This finding may not surprise you, but remember: many instructors and golfers emphasize the left side, arguing that it provides the power for a right-handed golfer. Our studies of the shoulders and hips showed that the right side is at least as active as the left and sometimes more so.

2. The hips initiate movement into the ball.

One of the questions we wanted to answer was, "Do the hips push you through the swing or do they pull you through?" This has to do with the timing of the swing on both sides, and it's pretty clear from the data that hip muscle activity is initiated before the upper body turns into the shot—in other words, the hips pull you through.

3. Trunk rotation and flexibility are crucially important.

The most noticeable difference we see on film when comparing professionals and amateurs is in trunk rotation (especially when the swing is viewed from above). We've noticed that older and less skilled players tend to get less than half the trunk rotation of a skilled or younger player. This lack of flexibility and strength is an important reason why people tend to play less well as they grow older, because they gradually lose the arc of motion which enables the body segments to transmit maximum velocity to the club head at impact.

Our stress on flexibility and trunk rotation isn't new, but this aspect of the golf swing hasn't received sufficient emphasis as far as determining how these affect where the ball goes and how consistently it goes there. Golfers give themselves a noticeable handicap by letting their available arc of motion diminish through lack of flexibility and by failing to realize the importance of body rotation. Why? Well, one way power in golf can be achieved is by rotating the body segments through space, and transferring energy from one segment to the next. If you diminish the space through which these segments move, you must use considerably more muscle power or effort to derive the same output.

This means that to get the same club head speed at impact, you must "muscle" the club, and that puts added stress on your muscles. As the round progresses, these muscles can't do it all, and they are prone to injury and hastened fatigue.

4. *Rely on the large muscles of the body to generate power.*

A closely related finding is that the large muscles in the body supply much of the power in a golf swing, and these muscles—especially in the hips (the abductors and extensors)—are quite active in a pro's swing. The hip muscles are the largest in the body and you must learn to use their potential power. Remember, a muscle's power is proportional to its cross-sectional area, meaning that the bigger it is, the more potential power it has. So you can see that no matter how strong your wrists and forearms are, they cannot substitute for the proper use of your hip muscles.

Our research has given us a keen appreciation for the contribution made by the trunk and lower body to what happens at impact. Thus we're encouraging all golfers to emphasize this part of the body instead of only forearms, wrists, and hands. For example, we notice that less skilled golfers tend to swing the club primarily with their arms, while failing to use the power available to them in their trunk, hips, and legs. The golfer who is a "hands-and-arms" swinger loses a tremendous amount of potential power by failing to get a good body turn that makes use of the large muscles of the body.

In our research lab, the more we learn about the body's linkage system—the timing and sequencing of the body's segments as it performs an athletic movement such as the tennis serve or baseball pitch—the more we appreciate the importance of the hips. Basically, power in golf comes sequentially, from the feet up as you rotate your body into the shot: energy is transferred starting from the legs through the hips to the upper trunk, then to the shoulders and out through the arms to the wrist and hands, and finally to the club itself. Understanding how energy is transferred through this chain of events is one thing: next you must master a swing that does the job for you, so that the club head speed at impact will produce the desired outcome.

5. Skilled players are more efficient at using their muscles.

Skilled golfers are extremely efficient at using their muscles and their whole body when swinging the club, which is consistent with what the Biomechanics Lab has learned while investigating other sports such as tennis, baseball, and swimming. When comparing the eight pros in this study with the amateurs tested to date, we've noted that the highly skilled players use a much lower percentage of their maximum muscular output potential as they swing.

6. The rotator cuff muscles in the shoulder play an important role.

Before we began investigating the golf swing, we knew from our research in baseball and tennis that the rotator cuff is much more important than previously thought in these activities. It was interesting to confirm for golf the similarly important role of the rotator cuff muscles on both sides of the body. In fact, the rotator cuff muscles in the shoulder need to be stretched and strengthened separately, with special exercises that are different from those done for the rest of the arm.

Typical shoulder exercises primarily work the deltoids, but we know from our research that this muscle, which lies along the top of the shoulder, is relatively "silent" during a golf swing, while the rotator cuff muscles are active.

Once having completed his research, Dr. Jobe and his staff at the Centinela Hospital Medical Center developed a series of golf-specific exercises that would be effective for a professional golfer as well as a weekend player. According to Dr. Jobe, "Our basic concern was to give golfers a conditioning program that would improve their strength and flexibility, thus lowering their risk of injury."

The exercises developed by Dr. Jobe are now used by most of the players on the Senior Tour, as well as the regular PGA Tour and the LPGA Tour. Bruce Crampton, for one, works out regularly at the mobile training centers, and credits the fitness center as having helped his game tremendously, especially in regards to being positive about his game.

"The body is probably the most sophisticated piece of machinery that's known," Crampton says, "and every part of it needs to be worked, including your brain. By doing daily stretching and flexibility exercises in the fitness center, I'm also exercising my brain because I'm making it send the correct messages to my extremities. That helps me intellectually. My brain gets bigger and it gives me greater thinking power. They've proved that in the mobile unit, and I've had doctors confirm it."

Bobby Nichols agrees that the fitness center has helped to keep the players playing. "Golf is a very unorthodox game that creates a lot of strange positions for your body. When you swing the golf club, you're likely to pull a muscle or tear a ligament. When we work with the guys in the fitness trailer, they're able to get us right back into the game. We don't have to take a week off. They can get most of us back to feeling capable of playing within a one-to-

(Fig. 1.) *The Player Fitness Center, a mobile gym, follows the Senior Tour.*

two-day period. They have been a big boost for all of us senior players.'' (Fig. 1.)

For the last two years the man on tour responsible for the fitness center is Paul Schueren, a physical therapist and golfer who loves being on tour with professionals. Schueren is in the mobile center at the tournament site before seven o'clock, and he or his partner will stay until the last golfer comes off the course, usually between six and seven in the evening.

Schueren and the mobile fitness center travel for five to six weeks in a row, take one week off, and then return to the tour, averaging thirty to thirty-five tournaments a year.

The therapists usually see a professional who needs their help before he plays, give anyone some sort of heat or stretching exercise, and then after a round, when an ice treatment might be added to the normal stretch exercises, depending on the condition of the injury.

For the professionals on tour, Schueren recommends a stretching program which they can do in their hotel or at the mobile center. He also develops a flexibility program, as well as one for strength and endurance, using the bikes, weights, and other gym equipment.

Schueren, who has worked with other forms of professional athletics, believes that golfers are better athletes than people give them credit. "People who don't know golf think that it is easy to hit a ball and walk around a golf course. These players are playing eighteen holes of golf six days a week. They are also on the practice tee hitting several buckets of balls, taking perhaps two to three hundred swings a day.

"They are not like football players in terms of bulk, or a baseball player in terms of the ability to do short bursts and wind sprints, but they need to retain a good amount of flexibility in their backs and shoulders and hips in order to keep playing competitively."

For the weekend golfer, Schueren recommends an exercise program that starts with flexibility and endurance, and then works up to strength. And for proper exercises for a golfer, he recommends Dr. Jobe's book, *30 Exercises for Better Golf*, which is available from Champion Press of Centinela Hospital Medical Center in Inglewood, California 90307.

These exercises, according to Schueren, were developed

from the research findings. "We created flexibility exercises for the lower and upper back. Also we have exercises for the hips and hamstrings and also the shoulder area. The main purpose of all of these exercises is to keep the muscles flexible."

And the main purpose of the player fitness center on tour is to keep the golf pros in shape and playing. And that is exactly what it does.

Playing Clinic

Q. Why is golf such a great game?

A. Because it is like life itself. It picks you up or lets you down, depending on whether you've made the shot or not. Or had a good round. You can't look into the future and know what's going to happen on the golf course, nor can you do that in life. Golf is played one shot at a time. Life is played one day at a time.   BRUCE CRAMPTON

Q. Do you ever master the game of golf?

A. No, I don't think so. I'm eighty-five years old and have been a professional since I was eighteen, and I'm still trying to get it right.   HARRY COOPER

Q. What's the best way of getting the correct grip on a club?

A. Put the left hand on the club first so that you can lift it with just the index finger and thumb. Close the fingers of the left hand around the club and place the left thumb slightly to the right side of the shaft, as you look down on it. You should now be able to see two knuckles on the back of the left hand. The V formed by the thumb and the index finger is pointing to your right shoulder. Next, position the right hand with the palm facing the target. The right-hand grip is kept in the fingers, not the palm. The right hand overlaps the left hand, and the right little finger fits into the groove between the left index finger and middle finger. The right thumb folds over to the left side of the shaft as you look down on it.   BOBBY NICHOLS

Q. How fast should I swing the club?

A. Never rush a shot. The club speed builds up gradually through the swing and reaches its maximum at impact. The key is accelerating through the shot. Don't slow your backswing down or be slow at the top because then the tendency is to jump at the ball. Gradually build up swing speed throughout the shot.   BRUCE CRAMPTON

Q. Is there more than one good golf swing?

A. Of course. Just look at the likes of Lee Trevino, Walter Hagen, or Jack Nicklaus. There is no perfect swing. All that matters is the grip and the address. Make your own swing as simple a physical movement as you can. Then go practice that swing.   HARRY COOPER

Q. How can I gain control over a particular shot?

A. Practice. I've learned that muscles don't have memory, but the brain learns to fire the muscles in the correct order. You can create the feeling of what is right. You will learn the correct hitting position and where your hands should be at all times on a particular shot.
BRUCE CRAMPTON

Q. How far should I take the driver back in my swing?

A. The parallel position at the top of the swing is far enough. You tend to lose your grip if you go back any farther than that.   BRUCE CRAMPTON

Q. Should I have the same swing for all clubs?

A. I do. I use basically a three-quarter swing on my woods and irons. And I place the ball more or less from the same position in my stance.   BILLY CASPER

Q. What is your opinion of the new design in golf architecture?

A. Oh, don't get me started on that. I think all these new target courses are much too difficult for the average player. They are doing golf a disservice.   GENE LITTLER

Q. I'm having trouble with the long iron. What should I do?

A. You might think of getting rid of the two-iron and replace it with a five-wood. The new metal woods give a player a bigger hitting area and are easier to hit.   BILLY CASPER

Q. How hard should I hit the ball?

A. Hit the shot from within yourself. Never stretch your abilities or your strength.   BRUCE CRAMPTON

Q. How much time should I spend practicing?

A. Go to the practice tee to develop a swing you can trust. Go to the golf course to develop the confidence you need to play. If you are a good player already, spend more time on the golf course than on the practice tee. However, always loosen up before you play.   HARRY COOPER

Q. Is the long putter for everyone?

A. It is, I think, for players who find that their left hand is breaking down on their regular putting stroke. And for the golfer who has developed the "yips."

BRUCE CRAMPTON

Q. How should I exercise for the game?

A. Start by doing flexibility exercises and then move toward endurance and building up your strength.

PAUL SCHUEREN

Q. How do I keep from topping the ball?

A. Make sure your knees are flexed; that will keep you down on the ball.   BOBBY NICHOLS

Q. What creates power in the swing?

A. The hips and shoulder turn with an extended arc. The longer the arc, the more power.   BOB WATSON

Q. How can an average golfer improve his game?

A. Take some lessons from a PGA professional. He'll get your score down.   HARRY COOPER

Q. How many events are on the Senior Tour?

A. Forty-one events are scheduled for 1990. We started with two in 1980. Not bad for one decade. BOB GOALBY

Q. How far away from the ball should I stand?

A. Make sure your arms are extended but you're not stretching for the ball.   HARRY COOPER

*Q. What happens when you lose your
    feel for the golf swing?*

A. We all do that. You just have to go back out onto the practice tee and search for it. You'll find it. BILLY CASPER

Q. How do I keep from steering the putt?

A. Get square to the cup. Focus on the back portion of the ball, and then hit through the putt. GENE LITTLER

*Q. How do I keep from topping the ball
    on a downhill lie?*

A. Play the ball back in the stance. Keep your hands slightly ahead. BOB GOALBY

Q. How far do you hit your irons today?

A. I'm hitting the same iron from the same distance that I did thirty years ago. I hit the seven-iron from 150 yards and a five-iron from 175. All that is different is that today we have better equipment. GENE LITTLER

Q. If I am just off the green, what should I use?

A. In the new, thicker fringe, I'd use the wedge and blade the shot. BOB GOALBY

Q. How can I improve my putting?

A. Go to school while your playing partners putt. Learn how to read the greens, to see which way the grass is growing. And then, when you step over the putt, just get comfortable, then stroke the ball smoothly. GENE LITTLER

*Q. What should I do if I get into a bad lie,
    either in the trap or rough?*

A. You first want to get the ball out of trouble. Pick the club for that purpose. Don't worry about distance.

BOB GOALBY

Q. Where can I find out which weight and shaft of club is best for me?

A. Go to a PGA golf shop and a PGA professional. They're trained to help you select the right equipment.

BOB WATSON

Q. Besides the fundamentals, what else should you take into consideration when you are about to hit a shot?

A. The wind, hazards, and the next shot. I want to position this shot so that I have a chance of scoring with the next one. That's simple golf-course management.

BILLY CASPER

Q. Do I need to buy all the clubs I see in a professional's bag?

A. Perhaps not every one. Also, many pros play with clubs that are less than "standard," and that's one reason they go farther than the average player's. But to be serious about golf, you need a full set. At least four woods, eleven irons, including a sand wedge and a pitching wedge. And, of course, a putter.

BILLY CASPER

Q. How can I calculate distance?

A. All professionals "walk" the course before they play. Or their caddie does it for them. Today, almost every course has a 150-yard marker to the green. Learn what to hit from that distance, and you'll develop your feel of what to hit from other distances. And naturally, if you play the same course, you'll quickly learn all the distances and which club to hit. BOBBY NICHOLS

Q. How far should I take the long irons
   back at the top of the swing?

A. I still use my three-quarter swing, and I think that works best for the average golfer as well. BILLY CASPER

Q. What's the most important part of
   any golf swing?

A. The first ten inches. The greatest player in the world is Jack Nicklaus, and he establishes his tremendous swing in the first foot. It all happens there: the club head speed, timing, and tempo. HARRY COOPER

Q. What's the secret of playing well out of sand?

A. To be a good bunker player, you need to know how to judge sand by simply walking into a trap and testing it. That's all it takes. Hitting from the sand is an easy shot. JIM FERREE

Q. How do I get backspin, especially on chip shots?
A. Hit down and cut across the ball. GENE LITTLER

Q. What are the advantages of the long putter?
A. It allows a person to stand taller at the ball and also permits a freer swing. It also, I'm sure, has an enormous psychological benefit for many players, especially those of us who have developed the "yips." BOB WATSON

*Q. How long do you think all of these
   seniors will keep playing golf?*

A. For as long as they can keep teeing it up, and as long
as anyone wants to come watch us play. We could go on
forever.   BILLY CASPER

Senior PGA Tour

MONY Senior Tournament of Champions
La Costa Country Club, Carlsbad, CA

\# + **Senior Skins Game**
Mauna Lani Resort, Hawaii

Royal Caribbean Classic
Key Biscayne Golf Course, Key Biscayne, FL

GTE Suncoast Classic
Tampa Palms Country Club, Tampa, FL

Aetna Challenge
The Club at Pelican Bay, Naples, FL

\#**Chrysler Cup**
Tournament Players Club at Prestancia, Sarasota, FL

Vintage Chrysler Invitational
The Vintage Club, Indian Wells, CA

Vantage at The Dominion
The Dominion Country Club, San Antonio, TX

\#*****Fuji Electric Grand Slam**
Oak Hill Country Club, Narita, Japan

The Tradition at Desert Mountain
Desert Mountain Golf Club, Scottsdale, AZ

PGA Seniors Championship
PGA National, Palm Beach Gardens, FL

#Liberty Mutual Legends of Golf
Barton Creek Country Club, Austin, TX

Murata Reunion Pro-Am
Stonebriar Country Club, Dallas, TX

Las Vegas Senior Classic
Desert Inn & Country Club, Las Vegas, NV

Southwestern Bell Classic
Quail Creek Golf and Country Club,
Oklahoma City, OK

Doug Sanders Kingwood Celebrity Classic
Deerwood Club, Houston, TX

Bell Atlantic Classic
Chester Valley Golf Club, Malvern (Philadelphia), PA

Nynex/Golf Digest Commemorative
Sleepy Hollow Country Club, Scarborough
(Tarrytown), NY

Mazda Senior TPC
Dearborn Country Club, Dearborn (Detroit), MI

MONY Syracuse Senior Classic
LaFayette Country Club, Syracuse, NY

Digital Seniors Classic
Nashawtuc Country Club, Concord (Boston), MA

Unofficial prize money
+ Four-player field
* Recognized event, but not part of 42-event official schedule

USGA Senior Open
Ridgewood Country Club, Ridgewood, NJ

Northville Long Island Classic
Meadow Brook Country Club, Jericho (Long Island), NY

Kroger Senior Classic
Jack Nicklaus Sports Center, Kings Island, OH

Ameritech Senior Open
Grand Traverse Resort, Traverse City, MI

Newport Cup
Newport Country Club, Newport, RI

PaineWebber Invitational (ESPN)
Tournament Players Club at Piper Glen, Charlotte, NC

Sunwest Bank/Charley Pride Senior Golf Classic
Four Hills Country Club, Albuquerque, NM

Showdown Classic
Jeremy Ranch Golf Club, Park City, UT

GTE Northwest Classic
Inglewood Country Club, Kenmore (Seattle), WA

GTE North Classic
Broadmoor Country Club, Indianapolis, IN

Vantage Bank One Classic
Kearney Hill Links, Lexington, KY

Greater Grand Rapids Open
Elks Country Club, Grand Rapids, MI

Crestar Classic
Hermitage Country Club, Richmond, VA

Fairfield Barnett Space Coast Classic
Suntree Golf Club, Melbourne, FL

Vantage Championship
Tanglewood Park, Clemmons (Winston-Salem), NC

Gatlin Brothers Southwest Golf Classic
Fairway Oaks Country Club, Abilene, TX

Transamerica Senior Golf Championship
Silverado Country Club, Napa, CA

Gold Rush at Rancho Murieta
Rancho Murieta Country Club, Sacramento, CA

Centinela Hospital Classic
Rancho Park Golf Club, Los Angeles, CA

#Du Pont Cup Japan vs USA Senior Golf Matches
Tournament Players Club at Batoh, Japan

GTE Kaanapali Classic
Royal Kaanapali Golf Club, Lahaina, HA

New York Life Champions
Hyatt Dorado Beach, Puerto Rico

Unofficial prize money

Built in 1965 by Dick Wilson, this championship course is traditional in design, with elevated greens, water coming into play on ten holes, and famous for its 17th, the "mile long," hole, which is over 590 yards and the par is only five.

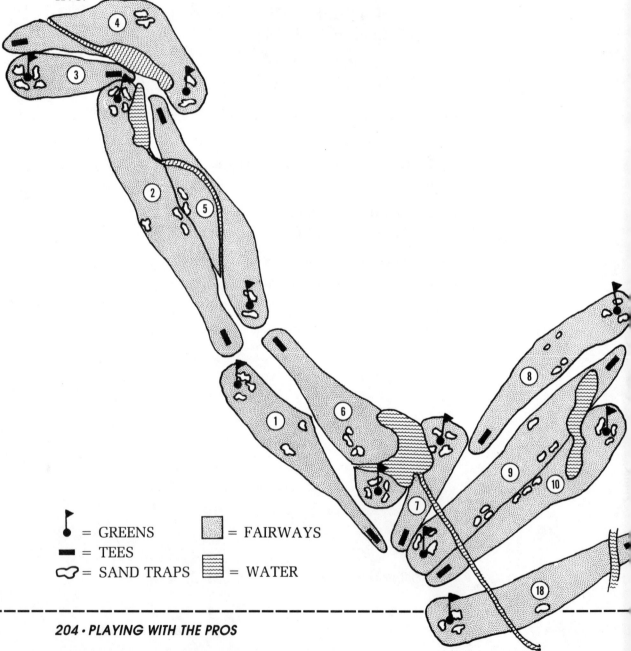

= GREENS   = FAIRWAYS
= TEES
= SAND TRAPS   = WATER

La Costa Country Club

HOLE	PAR	YARDS
1	4	412
2	5	526
3	3	187
4	4	386
5	4	446
6	4	365
7	3	188
8	4	398
9	5	538
OUT	36	3446
10	4	450
11	3	180
12	5	541
13	4	410
14	3	204
15	4	378
16	4	423
17	5	569
18	4	421
IN	36	3576
TOTAL	72	7022

TPC at Prestancia

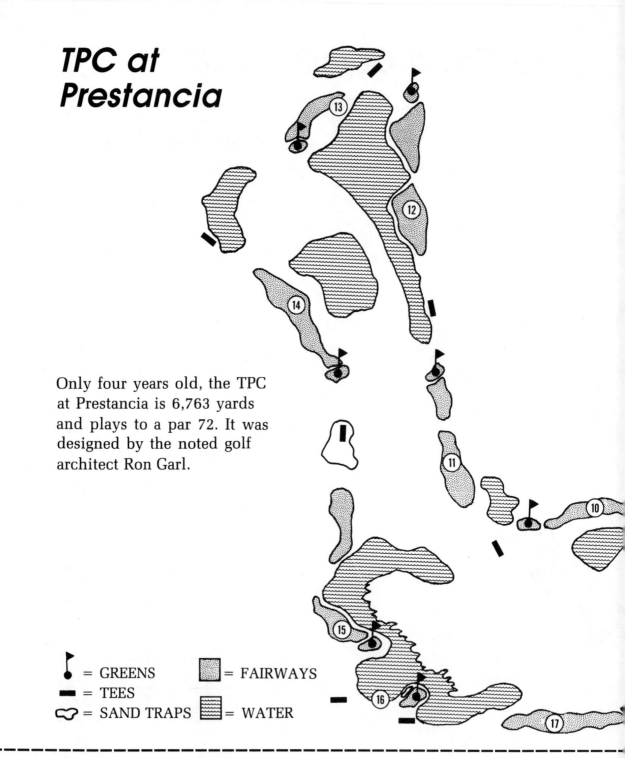

Only four years old, the TPC at Prestancia is 6,763 yards and plays to a par 72. It was designed by the noted golf architect Ron Garl.

🚩 = GREENS   ▦ = FAIRWAYS

▬ = TEES

◍ = SAND TRAPS   ▦ = WATER

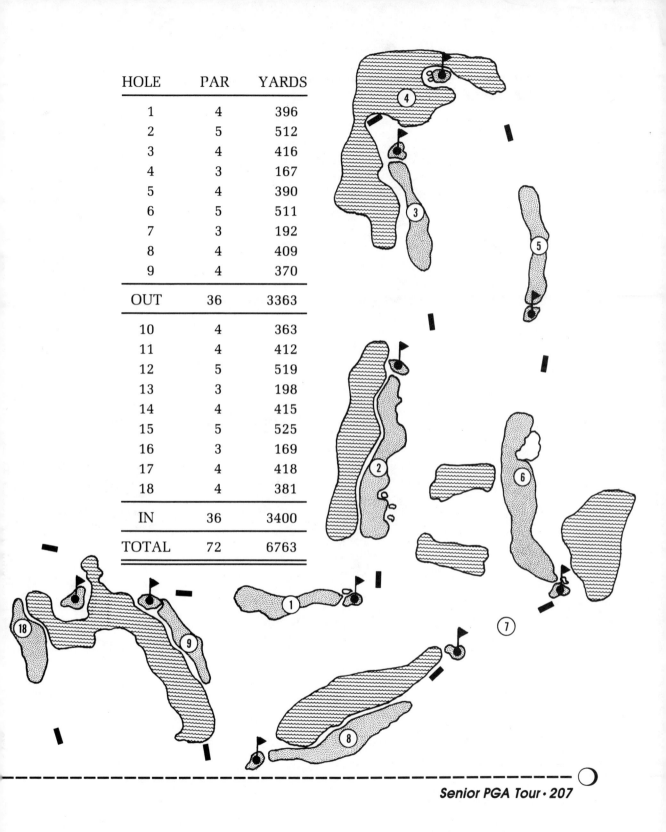

HOLE	PAR	YARDS
1	4	396
2	5	512
3	4	416
4	3	167
5	4	390
6	5	511
7	3	192
8	4	409
9	4	370
OUT	36	3363
10	4	363
11	4	412
12	5	519
13	3	198
14	4	415
15	5	525
16	3	169
17	4	418
18	4	381
IN	36	3400
TOTAL	72	6763

The Dominion

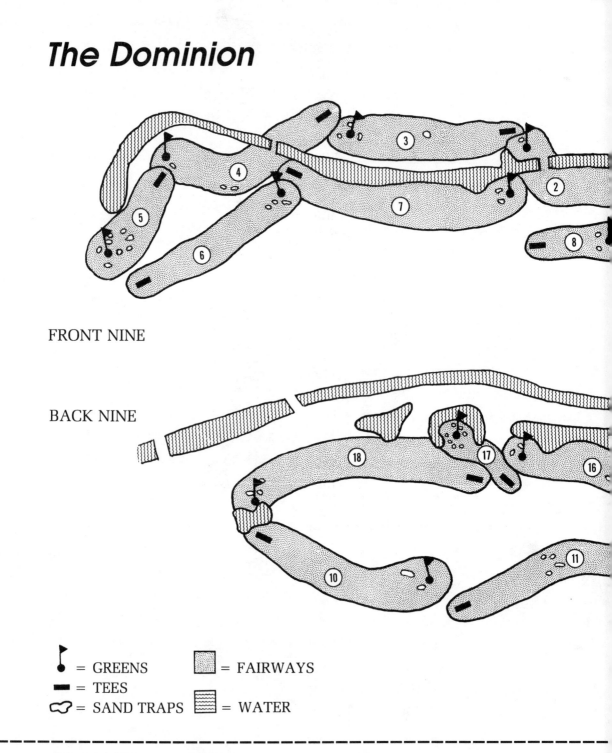

FRONT NINE

BACK NINE

= GREENS   = FAIRWAYS

= TEES

= SAND TRAPS   = WATER

The Dominion Country Club is a world-class golf course designed by Bill Johnston, a former Texas Open champion, who wanted a course that was "an improvement on nature itself" and a rewarding experience for players of all levels. The Dominion is both a breathtaking sight and a challenge to play.

HOLE	PAR	YARDS
1	4	413
2	4	363
3	4	385
4	4	405
5	3	202
6	4	360
7	5	538
8	3	189
9	5	488
OUT	36	3343
10	4	423
11	5	522
12	4	406
13	4	381
14	4	438
15	3	167
16	4	436
17	3	153
18	5	545
IN	36	3471
TOTAL	72	6649

Cochise

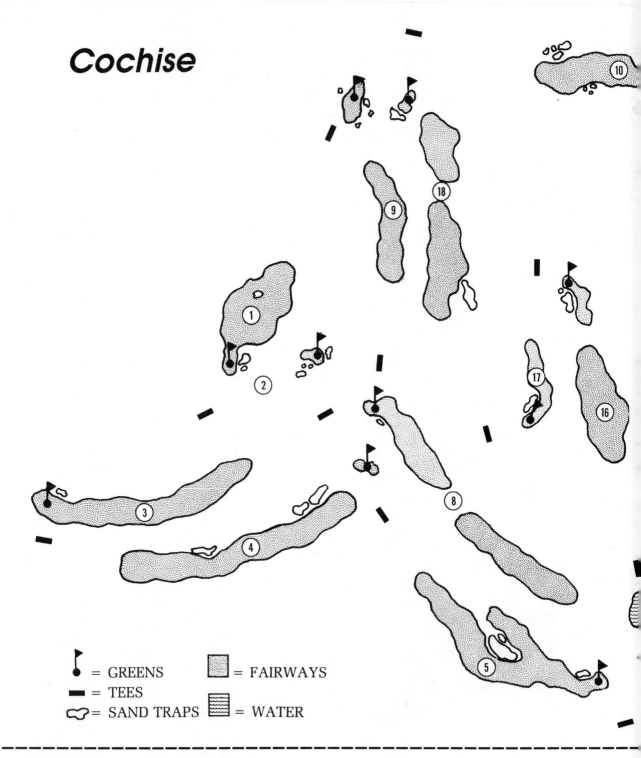

= GREENS
= TEES
= SAND TRAPS
= FAIRWAYS
= WATER

Cochise Course at Desert Mountain is one of the most picturesque courses in the world according to its designer, Jack Nicklaus. It was created to put a premium on good second shots and putting. Among the most memorable holes on Cochise are the par three 7th and the par five 15th. The greens for these two holes share an island approached from two different directions.

HOLE	PAR	YARDS	HOLE	PAR	YARDS
1	4	390	10	4	424
2	3	191	11	3	175
3	4	457	12	5	500
4	5	546	13	3	136
5	4	408	14	4	434
6	4	358	15	5	534
7	3	178	16	4	413
8	5	569	17	3	182
9	4	411	18	5	531
OUT	36	3508	IN	36	3329
			TOTAL	72	6837

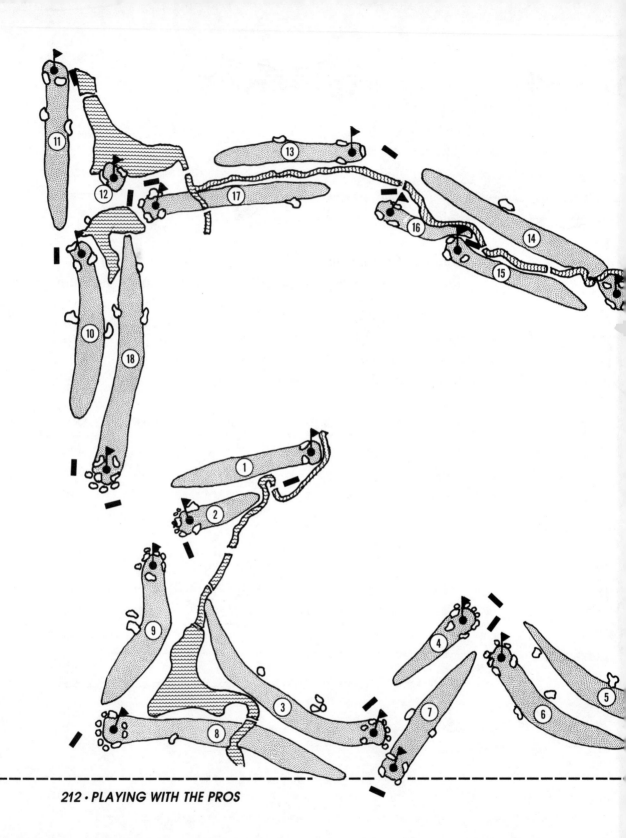

Quail Creek

Quail Creek Golf & Country Club course was designed by Floyd Farley and built in 1960. It is a challenge course of tight fairway, an abundance of overhanging trees, and over 75 extra large sand bunkers.

HOLE	PAR	YARDS
1	4	413
2	3	220
3	5	553
4	3	238
5	4	426
6	4	377
7	4	364
8	5	530
9	4	393
OUT	36	3514
10	4	431
11	4	425
12	3	180
13	4	418
14	5	587
15	4	386
16	3	206
17	4	469
18	5	515
IN	36	3617
TOTAL	72	7131

= GREENS
= TEES
= SAND TRAPS
= FAIRWAYS
= WATER

TPC at Piper Glen

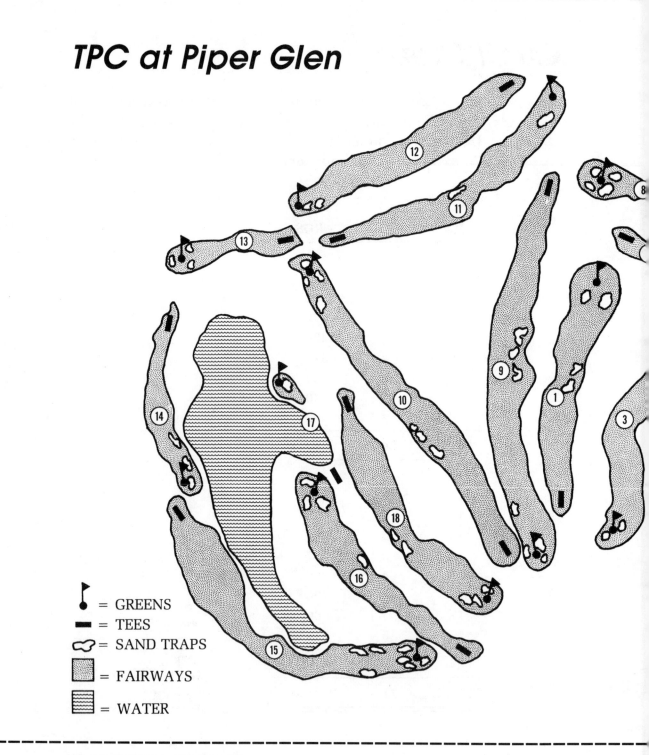

= GREENS

= TEES

= SAND TRAPS

= FAIRWAYS

= WATER

This Arnold Palmer-designed course opened in 1988. It is a hilly course of 6,853 yards and plays to a par 72. Cut out of a dense section of timber in the center of twelve hundred acres, over one thousand acres is used for fairways and greens, including a twenty-acre lake formed from an old quarry. Semi-island greens on the 17th and 18th are just two of the holes touched and surrounded by water. This is the first year for a Senior Tour event.

HOLE	PAR	YARDS
1	4	418
2	3	149
3	4	393
4	4	401
5	5	524
6	4	350
7	4	414
8	3	190
9	5	539
OUT	36	3378
10	5	574
11	4	391
12	4	428
13	3	192
14	4	328
15	5	522
16	4	403
17	3	197
18	4	413
IN	36	3448
TOTAL	72	6826

Jeremy Ranch Golf Club

= GREENS   = FAIRWAYS

= TEES

= SAND TRAPS   = WATER

Built in 1981 by Arnold Palmer and his chief architect, Ed Seay, this course of nearly 7,000 yards stretches over 1,000 acres of what once was a Utah sheep ranch.

HOLE	PAR	YARDS
1	4	375
2	4	431
3	5	531
4	3	196
5	4	458
6	4	432
7	4	369
8	3	196
9	5	478
OUT	36	3466
10	4	401
11	3	186
12	4	455
13	5	542
14	4	437
15	4	458
16	5	512
17	3	204
18	4	442
IN	36	3637
TOTAL	72	7103

Broadmoor Country Club

Broadmoor Country Club was designed in 1928 by the premier of the old-time Scottish golf course architects, Donald Ross. Jack Nicklaus says of Ross courses, "Other golf architects may lead a player to negative thinking. Donald Ross layouts lead to positive thinking. Everything looks so natural."

HOLE	PAR	YARDS
1	4	433
2	4	410
3	4	383
4	3	147
5	4	433
6	4	391
7	4	340
8	3	185
9	5	527
OUT	35	3249
10	4	403
11	3	198
12	5	567
13	5	482
14	4	400
15	3	155
16	4	364
17	5	482
18	4	395
IN	37	3446
TOTAL	72	6695

= GREENS   = FAIRWAYS
= TEES
= SAND TRAPS   = WATER

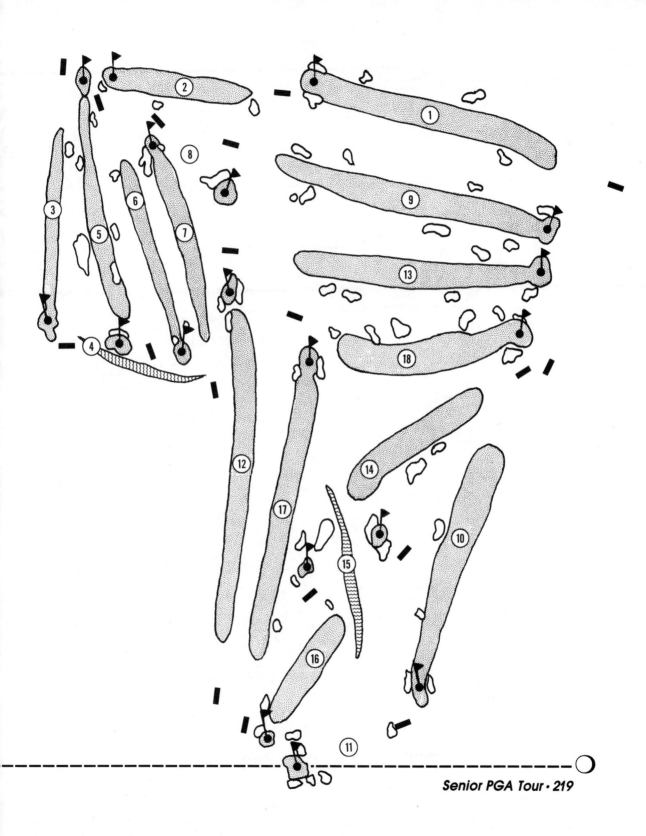

HOLE	PAR	YARDS			
			10	4	425
1	4	398	11	3	198
2	4	453	12	4	425
3	5	569	13	4	399
4	3	214	14	5	528
5	4	400	15	4	395
6	4	423	16	3	165
7	4	410	17	4	471
8	3	185	18	5	562
9	5	536	IN	36	3568
OUT	36	3588	TOTAL	72	7166

⚑ = GREENS

▬ = TEES

◠ = SAND TRAPS

▦ = FAIRWAYS

▩ = WATER

Fairway Oaks Country Club

The course opened in 1979, designed by Ron Garl with help from Senior Tour player, Charles Coody. It is well known for its 11 water holes and wide-open fairways.

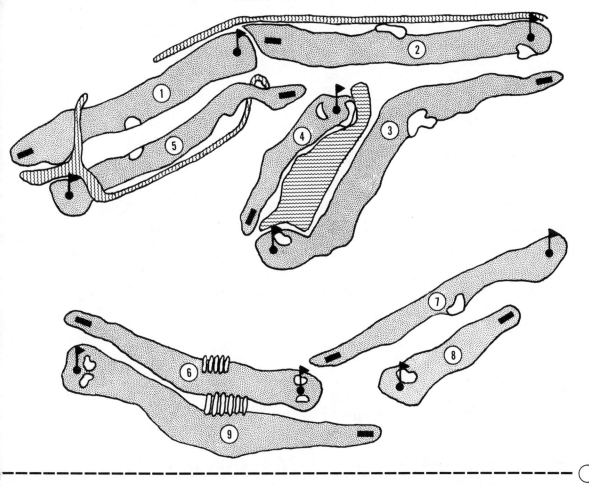

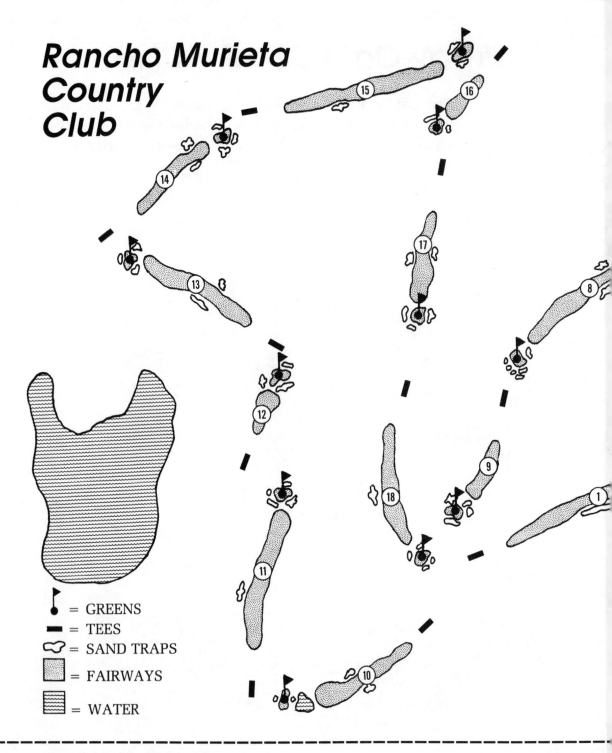

Rancho Murieta
Country
Club

● = GREENS

▬ = TEES

🌿 = SAND TRAPS

▨ = FAIRWAYS

▨ = WATER

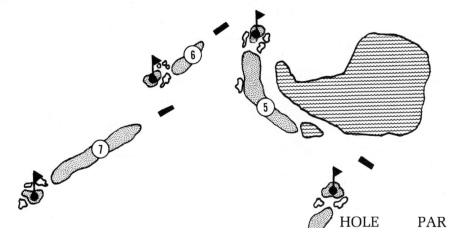

HOLE	PAR	YARDS
1	4	338
2	3	174
3	5	527
4	4	431
5	4	373
6	3	196
7	4	375
8	5	525
9	4	375
OUT	36	3314
10	4	406
11	5	490
12	3	170
13	4	435
14	4	360
15	5	560
16	3	167
17	4	370
18	4	429
IN	36	3387
TOTAL	72	6701

The Rancho Murieta Country Club is nestled in the foothills of California's historic Gold Country. It is the home of two championship courses, the newest being an Arnold Palmer-designed 6,875-yard, par 72 course.

Glossary

Address—Position assumed to hit the golf ball. Back is fairly straight and bent slightly from the hips. Feet are spaced the same as width of the shoulders. Body weight is distributed from the balls of the feet to the heels.

Apron—The two- or three-foot border around the green, slightly finer cut than fairway grass.

Birdie—One stroke under par.

Bogey—One stroke over par.

Bunker—Traditionally meant fairway trap, now means all sand traps.

Choking the club—Placing the hands one or more inches down the shaft of the club; used to control the golf club better.

Closed stance—Left foot is forward at the address and closed to the line of flight.

Divot—The turf cut from the ground under the ball.

Fade—The ball curves slightly from left to right in the course of the flight.

Fairway—The cut grass from tee to green where ball is to be played.

Firm left side—The straight but not stiff left arm, wrist, and leg. The golf swing begins with these key elements.

Flex—Refers to the stiffness of a club, and how far that stiffness will allow the club shaft to bend during the swing. Shafts come in four basic degrees of flex: X (extra-stiff), S (stiff), R (regular or medium), and L (ladies or flexible).

Golf clubs—There are three basic types of clubs: woods, irons, and the putter. All have heads, shaft, and a grip.

Grip—Leather end of the club shaft. Also, the position of one's hands on the club.

Hazard—Any natural part of the course that must be overcome or avoided: sand traps, water, trees.

Hook—The ball when driven curves to the left. A hooking ball has over-spin on it.

Irons—There are a total of eleven iron clubs, numbered one through nine plus the sand wedge and pitching wedge. The sand wedge has the more loft and a wider sole.

Lateral movement—A slide or shift of the majority of body weight from one side of the body to the other, but without a pivot.

Loft—Determines the trajectory that a golf ball will follow when hit with a particular club. Manufacturers have set a "standard" for all golf clubs, since no loft regulation exists in the rules of golf.

Long putter—An elongated, chest-high shafted putter which is used with a pendulum stroke.

Open stance—Left foot is pulled back off the line two or three inches.

Overlapping grip—Little finger of the right hand overlaps the forefinger of the left hand on the shaft of the club.

Over the top—The club approaches the ball from outside the target line and above the plane of the backswing.

Par—The score that a good golfer is expected to make on a given hole, and for eighteen holes.

Plugged—Ball is buried in deep sand.

Plumb putting—Using your dominant eye and vertical putter to determine the slope of a green.

Pivot—The turning of the body that coils the power. It is a movement of the body weight from left to right, then back again.

Pull—Means the same as hook, but usually the ball drifts to the left instead of curving.

Putter—Used almost exclusively for making rolling shots on the green. Putters come in all shapes, weights, and sizes.

Reading the green—Deciding which way the roll will break on the green.

Rough—High-cut grass bordering the fairway on both sides.

Slice—Ball curves to the left, usually dramatically.

Swinging plane—The level, or arc, of the swing, particularly the backswing.

Swing weight—The distribution of weight in a club.

Tee—The raised flat mound from which the drive is made.

Tempo—The steady speed or rhythm of the swing as a whole.

Tight Lie—Little room behind the ball in which to place the club.

Touch—An ability to "feel" how hard a putt should be hit. Also, the ability to play from around the green.

Trap shot—A shot from the sand, with either a wood or iron.

Unplayable lie—A ball in such a position that it can't be played.

Woods—The driver (one-wood) and the fairway woods (two-, three-, four- and increasingly the five-, six-, seven-). Traditional woods are made from persimmon or laminated maple. The new and popular metal "woods" are made mostly of stainless steel.